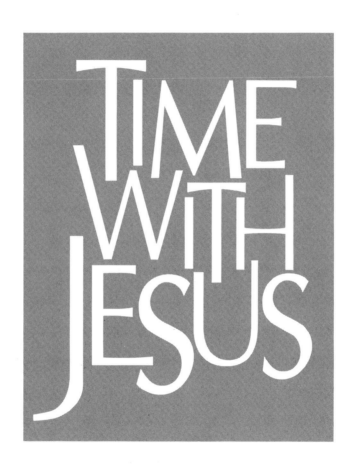

Twenty Guided Meditations for Youth

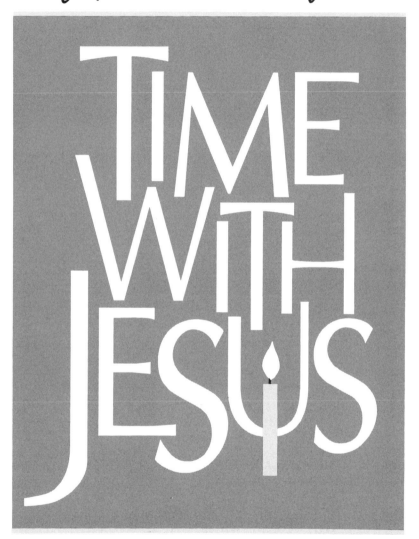

TIME WITH JESUS

THOMAS F. CATUCCI

AVE MARIA PRESS Notre Dame, Indiana 46556

Thomas Catucci is a priest of the Diocese of Syracuse New York where he is the director of Seminar House, a retreat facility serving primarily adolescents and young adults. He is the former Director for Formation for Youth Ministry for the Diocese. He has master's degrees in theology and scripture from the University of Buffalo; in Methodologies of Education and Developmental Theory in Education through the State University of New York and St. John Fisher College. He has done post-graduate work at Fordham, New York University and Boston College.

© 1993 by Ave Maria Press, Notre Dame, IN 46556

International Standard Book Number: 0-87793-499-1

Library of Congress Catalog Card Number: 93-71891

Cover and text design by Elizabeth J. French

Printed and bound in the United States of America.

Table of Contents

SECTION ONE: Four Relaxation Techniques

SECTION TWO: Twenty Guided Meditations

SECTION THREE: Four Responses

Introduction

Although the practice might seem unfamiliar, meditation is far more common than we think. Perhaps a person spends half an hour watching in silent admiration as the sun sinks slowly into the ocean or over the horizon, struck suddenly by a profound awareness of God's power. Perhaps, in the midst of personal crisis, a few quiet minutes are spent in the nearest chapel, watching flickering candlelight, breathing in the scent of wax and incense, searching the heart and pleading with God for peace. Most of us have at one time meditated on the action—or seeming inaction—of God in our lives, whether to offer grateful praise for recent blessings or to question the meaning of overwhelming trials.

At the same time, however, few people take the time to meditate deliberately. It is a form of prayer that, more often than not, catches us off guard. It is typically understood to be beyond the capacity of ordinary Christians, reserved for the exceptionally pious, such as those who have taken religious vows. Sometimes meditation is viewed with suspicion, as an unfamiliar practice of non-Christian religions. Such views miss the extraordinary rewards possible through the practice of meditation.

Within the church there is a rich tradition of meditation, beginning early when men and women withdrew from society, often establishing individual hermitages in the desert, seeking God in solitude, seeking escape from the distractions of society. Throughout history, saints such as Benedict, Teresa of Avila, Ignatius of Loyola, Francis de Sales, and other more anonymous figures, like the author of a very important book on meditation called *The Cloud of Unknowing*, have continued in the same tradition. They have taught us much through their lives and writings of the ways of meditation and of the benefits it offers to our relationship with our God. Thomas Merton and Pierre Teilhard de Chardin are more modern practitioners who have enriched us with their writings on the subject.

Much can be gained by introducing today's youth to this style of prayer. Teens often want an experience of God that is concrete, so that God seems more real to them. Yet so much of what we suggest meets with resistance because of boredom or the frustration that results from a sense of being "preached at."

They seek a God of power and love, one that can affect their lives and reshape them. They have heard of the power of the God of the holy scriptures. They've read all the stories, studied and memorized passages, and role-played the skits. But too frequently the God of the scriptures remains just printed words on paper, something to be talked about, a possibility rather than a reality. The craving that lingers in our teens is for a real experience, an intimate experience of the God who promised to remain with us.

If they experience for themselves the powerful sense of God's presence and love possible through meditation, they will be much more likely to continue on their own and strengthen their relationship with God throughout their lives. The challenge is simply to get them started, give them the opportunity to discover meditation and experience some of its benefits.

The next question then is "How?" Trying to explain meditation can be like trying to catch the wind. In most instances, meditation is something done in solitude, a problem for those of us who work with teens in groups of all sizes. And what is to prevent them from making use of a few quiet minutes intended for meditation for a quick nap instead? The answer lies in introducing teen-agers to guided meditation.

Rather than simply telling teens to try to relax and "think about" a certain prayer or scripture passage or phrase, it is more helpful to lead them through it, giving direction to their thought, helping them to keep focused on the prayer or passage intended for meditation. Many times teens do not know how to pray or, as they might say, "what to pray for." They lack experience, not through any failure on their part or their parents', but because they are just beginning to gain a capacity for more personal and intimate prayer.

As children, memorized prayers served them well but they outgrow them in their teen years. Just as they are seeking more intimate, interpersonal relationships with their peers, they are ready for a more intimate relationship with God. They just need to be shown how.

These guided meditations will help today's teens experience a new power in prayer. In my experience comments like these have become common: "I never felt so close to Jesus as I just did when we prayed." "Totally awesome." "For the first time in my life I really felt like I was communicating with the Lord." "It's almost like Jesus is really here to care for me and lead me." "I never thought prayer could be like this." Even the most reluctant and bored become inflamed and excited about their intimate experience of God.

The guided meditations in this book are able to affect the person who meditates in a great variety of ways, much as Jesus had varying effects on people in the scripture passages that inspired these meditations. The meditations become individual celebrations of deeper trust in God, of growth in faith, of new confidence and insight. And of course they become a celebration of Jesus' healing power in our own lives today.

How to Use This Book

Time With Jesus contains all the tools necessary for a leader of prayer to conduct effective guided meditations. Included are four relaxation techniques designed to help the participant prepare for meditation; the complete scripts for twenty scripturally-based guided meditations; and four responses designed to help the participants reflect on the experience. All that is required is a person of sensitivity and patience to read the scripts and guide the listeners in their prayer.

The book is organized around these components: Section One contains the relaxation techniques; Section Two, the guided meditations; and Section Three, the responses. These sections support one another and can be shuffled and matched to tailor each prayer encounter to your situation. Just make sure to choose a relaxation technique to prepare for the guided meditation and a response with which to follow it up.

Because the scripture passages that inspired these meditations are well-known, they are not reprinted here. However the citation is always provided at the beginning of each meditation, along with a brief description designed to assist you in making an appropriate choice for your group's time of prayer. Also included is a rough estimate of the time needed for each meditation. Don't forget to set aside time before and after for the relaxation technique and any response you want your youth to make.

As you select a meditation for a specific use, remember to be sensitive to the needs of your participants. Be sure to read the meditation completely before using it, keeping an eye out for potentially meaningless or overly painful passages for your participants. For example, if members of your group come from families going through divorce or separation, or suffering the recent loss of a parent or sibling, it might be best to avoid meditations that center around family life or memories of past holidays, birthdays, or family celebrations.

Remember too that some participants on any given day may not be able to relax or concentrate enough to stay with the process. Encourage the participants to try to stay with the meditation, but let them know that it's OK if someone finds it more difficult than usual to relax. Ask them to keep working on getting back into the meditation throughout the process. If they can't, allow them to let their thoughts wander where they will, but encourage them to respect the presence of those around them who are actively involved in the meditation.

None of these meditations needs to be used exactly as they are offered. Feel free to adapt or rephrase. If you feel up to the challenge, recreate a meditation to better accommodate your needs. If a section seems potentially painful or disturbing to some members of your group, consider omitting it if it won't harm the intent of the meditation. However, it is best to do this kind of work in advance, writing out the changes that you have made so that you do not have to improvise during the meditation and risk breaking its rhythm and flow.

The guided meditations have been created to impact on a variety of levels: physical (incorporating all the senses), intellectual, emotional, spiritual, and psychological—in the manner that Jesus addressed those who approached him.

All these scripts have been written with the listener in mind. Because they are meant to be read aloud, a great deal of attention has been given to word sounds, the flow of the text, rhythm, and continuity. You can make the most of these aspects of the text by keeping in mind a few simple tips:

—Read slowly. Pauses are written into the text for quiet reflection (…). Those sections followed by a longer space allow the meditator more time for silent conversation. Do not be afraid of, or rush through, the silent spaces.

—Read with little inflection. A very dramatic reading can be its own distraction. Read beyond a monotone, but try to keep your tone relaxing and conducive to prayer. At times the meditation is written almost as a drone. This allows the meditators to begin to anticipate what will be said, so that they can briefly let go of the distraction of your voice and enter more deeply into their prayer. At other times, it is intended that the meditation have a lulling effect, usually an indication of a common pause.

—Read with cadence. After familiarizing yourself with a specific meditation you have chosen, you will recognize its natural rhythm. Flow with that rhythm.

—Read with confidence. Before you begin remind yourself of the opening prayer which always requests the active presence of the Holy Spirit. The participant is always in the gentle hands of the Lord during this prayer. God will accomplish so much more than any words written or spoken on God's behalf. Be confident in your role as reader and in the role of the Holy Spirit.

Meditative prayer, which is an internal experience of God, can become diverted by the onslaught of sensory information. Spiritual guides usually address this problem by simply stating that the preparation for prayer requires "moving toward quiet." They tell us that this can be achieved by entering the stillness within ourselves and concentrating on that inner place where the Spirit of God dwells. This can be difficult to achieve since even unconsciously we continue to analyze our external surroundings by catching each sound, flicker, waft, and texture.

There are some simple things we can do to help achieve the kind of recollection and freedom from distraction that is necessary for meditation. The following three suggestions offer practical assistance in making the transition from a natural focus on outside stimuli to an awareness of the workings of our inner selves. Before you begin to lead your group through a meditation, go over the following points with them:

—Find a sacred space. The location for prayer is often as important as the prayer itself. A sacred environment seems to frame the meditation with an immediate presence of God. Moving to a new location at the outset can create a sense that what follows is different, special, and set aside from everything else. It is important to find an area free from visual distractions; dimming the lights can also help to create a conducive atmosphere.

—Listen to the silence. We are often afraid of silence, hiding from it with radios, televisions, and sound systems. When silence is forced on us, it is often broken with nervous laughter, whispering, or countless other distractions. Meditation, however, requires silence. It should begin as soon as the sacred space is entered and should not be broken until after the response is completed.

To counter distracting noises that cannot be controlled, try "white noise," like the steady hum of a fan running. Music can also be used to block unwanted noises. And it can enhance a meditation. The best music I have found is by contemporary composers such as Kitaro.

—Find a comfortable posture. During meditation, the body should rest while the mind works. Be cautious of reclining fully, however, since it's too easy to fall asleep in that position. On the other hand don't specify rigid positions. I've heard from too many people who report spending most of their meditation time concentrating on whether or not they were in the correct, official position.

Once you have reviewed these points with your participants, and they have arranged themselves accordingly, you will be ready to begin.

Section One

Four Relaxation Techniques

The following four relaxation techniques are designed to prepare the participants for prayer and for the main experience of the meditation itself. All of these seek to move us to the inside of ourselves and to activate the imagination and the senses. Each technique focuses on a different route to achieve this.

As you read through them, remember they are intended to help the participants relax and open themselves to the experience of God in their lives and hearts. Some techniques may be suitable for some participants but not for others. Relaxation One, for example, which leads the listener into an examination of how well and how beautifully all of the parts of the body work independently and together, may not be appropriate if your group includes any who are physically challenged. Choose the technique carefully, being sensitive to the lives of your participants, so that the experience will be as relaxing as possible for all. Remember that, as with the meditations, you may adapt these to suit your group.

Each meditation should begin with one of the four relaxation scripts. Although there is a suggested relaxation script for each meditation, it is not necessary to adhere to these suggestions. If you plan to use the meditations on a regular basis, you may want to consider using the same relaxation script the first few times; a growing sense of familiarity may help new participants to feel more comfortable with the process, resulting in a richer experience of prayer.

Focusing the Physical Body for Prayer

This relaxation technique focuses the five senses on our own bodies, helping us to connect with the image and likeness that we bear to God. It is through this God-created form that the Lord comes to us and goes out to others. Time: 3.5 minutes

Gently close your eyes …
And block out everything around you …
Just relax and be still …
With your eyes closed … focus on your feet …
Wiggle your toes …
These are strong feet … feet that God created just for you …
Feet that have felt the cool, wet sand at the beach …
Feet that have felt the damp softness of fresh cut grass in the spring …
Feet that have felt warm, squishy mud ooze up between the toes after a
    summer rain …
Good feet … strong feet … feet that God will use …

Now with your eyes still closed … feel your legs …
Strong legs … sturdy legs that God has given you …
Legs that have climbed hills …
Legs that have peddled a bike …
Legs that have run and skated …
Good legs … strong legs … legs that God will use …

And now just relax …
Concentrate on your arms …
Strong arms …
Arms that have carried groceries …
Arms that have dug in the garden …
Arms that have shoveled the snow …
Arms that are strong enough to work hard …
And gentle enough to wrap around someone you love …
Strong arms … gentle arms …
Arms that God will use to love others with …
Relax … relax and be at peace …

Concentrate on your hands ...
Hands that are strong ... strong to do housework ...
Strong to wash and to clean ...
Hands that have written papers ... dried dishes ... combed hair ...
Hands that God has used to plant seeds ... to write love letters ...
Hands strong enough to scrub and polish ... and gentle enough to
    wipe away tears ...
Strong hands ... gentle hands ... hands that God will use ...
Be at peace ... and relax ...

Concentrate on your ears ... and all they've heard ...
Ears that God has used to hear the songs of birds returning home in the
    spring ...
Ears that have heard the laughter of children in a playground ...
The thunder of waves on the shore ... of water falling into a lagoon ...
Have heard the beauty of music ... the sound of night crickets ...
The harmony of laughing friends ...
And the tender whisper of an "I love you" ...
And be at peace.

Think of your eyes and all they have seen ...
The rainbow splashed against a fresh washed sky ...
Eggs hatching with new life ...
Snow drifting and covering the earth ...
The softness of fog drifting over a lake ...
Tulips opening in the morning sunrise ...
The gifts of God ... the eyes to see the gifts ...
And be at peace ... at peace.

And we pray ...

Letting Our Breath Lead Us to Prayer

Using breathing techniques to prepare for prayer, we parallel our breathing to the breath of God. This exercise helps us to slowly and gently become receptive to God's Spirit. Time: 3 minutes

Gently close your eyes and imagine a smooth, quiet wind ...
    blowing against a sail on a boat ...
Pushing ... moving ...
Imagine the city skyline ... and the wind twisting smoke from a chimney ...
So slow ... so lazy ... drifting ...
Feel the soft ... clear wind against your face ...
Drifting over your eyes ... against your temples ... through your hair ...
Like a breath ... over you ... around you ... lifting you ...

Bring the breath into you ...
Silently ... through your nose ... fill yourself with that sweet breath ...
And hold it for a few seconds ...
Let it become part of you ...
Then silently ... push it from you through your mouth ...
Slowly ... silently ...

Again ... bring the soft breath deep within ...
Silently ... feel your body fill ...
Hold it a few moments ...
And this time ... attach any distractions or uninvited thoughts to the breath
    and quietly push them out ... together ... through your mouth ...
Quietly ... let go ...

Now think of this breath as the breath of God ...
Pure ... clean ... life-giving ...
Breathe in the breath of life from God ...
And hold it a few seconds ...
Fill yourself ...
Now push out any pains or hurts that are inside ...
Slowly ... gently ... quietly ...
Gently push them ... and let them go ...

Now … breathe in God's healing …
His power to make new and clean …
Breathe in God's wholeness …
God's soothing purity …
Let it become part of you …
Saturate you …
And silently breathe out any anger you may have …
Let the anger go out with your breath …
Slowly … softly … gently.

Another deep breath …
This time bring in God's love …
Draw God's love into you with your breath …
God's breath …
Let that love from God soak into every muscle and cell …
Bathe yourself in God's love …
Let his love flow into every part of you that needs him …
And relax …
Be still within …
And breathe slowly … quietly … softly …
And feel the presence of God's being …
Radiating within …
Warming you within …
Filling you within …

And we pray …

Relaxation Technique Three

Journey Back in Time

Time jumping can be disjointing for the meditating mind. Here is a preparation for meditation that helps the young mind to adjust slowly and move smoothly from the here-and-now to the time of Christ, several thousand years ago. Time: 4 minutes

Gently close your eyes …
Be comfortable … relaxed …
Take a deep, silent breath and settle yourself …

With your eyes closed …
Take a journey …
Imagine yourself comfortably seated in a big, clear bubble …
Safe … secure … nothing can harm you …
Things can change outside the bubble …
But not within … everything within remains the same … constant …
And the bubble can travel …
Relax … be at peace … and feel the wonder …

The bubble will take you back in time …
Safely … gently … slowly …
With your eyes still closed …
Go back to last summer …
The warmth of the sun …
The smell of suntan lotion …
Friends getting together … a picnic … a party …

Keep going back …
Back to Christmas … several years ago …
See the tree … the gifts … the lights shining brightly …
Smell the cinnamon and eggnog … taste the cookies and candy canes …
Remember your family … a hug … someone who cares …
And be at peace … restful … quiet …

Travel still further back …
You are in the third grade … standing in line …
Boys on one side … girls on the other …
You are playing kick ball … singing … making up silly skits …

21

Handing out valentines ...
Making a gift for Mother's Day ... and Father's Day ...
Be at peace ... feel the peace ... remember the fun ...

And continue back ... further back in time ...
You are an infant ... cradled in your mother's arms ...
Snuggled in a warm blanket ...
She holds you tightly ... close to her ... safe ... secure ...
Nothing can harm you ...
Safe ... peaceful ... gentle ...

But keep going back in time in your bubble ...
To the early days of our country ...
With your eyes closed ... go back to the American Revolution ...
The signing of the Declaration of Independence ...
And now travel to the crossing of Christopher Columbus ...
In the middle of the ocean ... on one of the three ships ...
Feel the rocking of the boat ... smell the salty water ...

And keep going back in time ...
You rise ... lift up ... fly ...
Across the Atlantic ... through the Straits of Gibraltar ...
Now you are moving very quickly ...
Past Spain ... over the northern coast of Africa ...
Past Morocco ... slow down a little over Egypt ...
You can see the Nile River with all the boats ...
The pyramids of the pharaohs ... the huge temples ...
Parades of flowers ... the bright sun and gentle palms ...
Barefoot people in white gauze ... carrying baskets ...
Now continue flying along the coast ...
Into the desert region of Israel ... the Holy Land ...
Where even the ground is sacred ...
Where God has met his people ... where God has spoken ...
And now rest ... settle down on the sacred earth ...
And be at peace ... settle and rest ... wait ... at peace ...

And we pray ...

Floating on Grace

Grace has often been compared to an ocean that laps a floating iceberg, slowly melting and dissolving it so that the two forms of water may be united. This relaxation technique transforms that image as if the individual were slowly walking into a lake, and then swimming, and finally floating in God's love. Time: 3 minutes

Look around you … and then settle in …
Relax … and feel the quiet …
Slowly close your eyes … and feel the stillness …
Become part of the quiet …
Enter into the silence … and become part of it …
Rest … peacefully … silently …

And with your eyes closed …
Drift … to a place far away …
Drift in your imagination …
To a large body of water …
A gentle body of water …
That laps the shore lazily …
Slowly lapping … and lapping …
The water slowly rising … and sliding across the shore …
Then withdrawing … and sliding back …

Look at the ripples of the surface …
Moving so slowly … so gently …
Now slowly take a small step forward …
Put your foot into the water …
It almost tickles …
But there is no sense of it being cold …
And it has no feeling of being warm …
It's the same temperature as you …
And the only feeling is one of pleasure …
As if wherever you place your foot … the water conforms to
    your shape … and fits … comfortably …

And with another small step …
You realize that it really isn't water …

23

It's thicker …
And it conforms to you …
It seems to hold you up … making you feel lighter …
Another step … slowly … and you're up to your knees …
It feels dry … and buoyant … but it still moves and sparkles like water …
Still lapping near the shore …
Lapping against you … so very gently …
And there is a great feeling of peace … and solitude …
And comfort …
Comfort …

And take yet another step … and another …
Until you're up to your waist …
But you feel incredibly buoyant …
Almost weightless … like a balloon …
Slowly gliding into the sea …
And with great courage …
You let go …
Slowly lean down … and push off … as if you would swim …
But it seems impossible to sink …
You feel as if something is holding you up … like a bubble …
And you roll over on your back … look up into blueness …
With no effort … you float … and feel very light … almost suspended …
You can close your eyes … and drift … slowly drift …
And as it laps against you so gently …
You can feel it slowly melting away the pressures … the tensions …
    the worries …
And you feel yourself gently bobbing … the cares and worries melting away
    … and your spirit is free …
Drifting … slowly … relaxed … carefree … and weightless.

And we pray …

Section Two

Twenty Guided
Meditations

The Birth of Christ

With the simplicity and wonder of the shepherds, we find God, who is one like us, born of the flesh. Inspired by Luke 2:6-20. The use of relaxation technique three is suggested. Time: 11 minutes

And we pray:
Lord Jesus Christ …
Be with us as we meditate …
Guide us in our prayer …
For we trust in you …
And in your Holy Spirit directing our thoughts and our dreams to
    discover you in our lives …
Be with us Lord …
Guide us in peace …
Stay near …
Be near …

With your eyes still closed …
Travel past the sunset …
Into the darkness of a winter night in ancient Israel …
Gliding over a huge desert … you can see a large cliff ahead of you …
Come to rest on that cliff … overlooking the desert …
You are alone …
And very safe …
And nothing can harm you …

The heat of the desert day has cooled …
It's winter … but still warm …
Feel how pleasantly comfortable you are …

Look around you …
Ahead of you is the vast expansive desert …
Outlined in moonlight …
If you look with care … the darkness of the night is broken with a slight
    glow at the horizon … the final curtain of the day …
Breathe deeply … notice how clean the air is … how clear … how sweet …
Overhead you can see a multitude of stars … so many stars …

As if you are standing in the middle of ... and yet beneath ...
    all the constellations ...
Clusters of stars twinkle and blink above you ...

Turn around and see the most wondrous gathering of stars imaginable ...
There ... to your right ...
A star that seems brighter than the rest ... near the horizon ...
As if four or five stars cluster together ...
An incredibly bright mark in the sky ...
One or two stars in the cluster ... seem to hang a little lower than the others ...
As if pointing to the earth ...
Pointing to someplace in the desert ...
They blink ... they pulse ... as if they want you to notice something special ...

You search ...
Leaving the cliff ... lifting up from the ground ... gliding toward those bright
    stars on the horizon ...
Follow your instinct ... follow your curiosity ... follow the star ...
Look down and notice a few tents huddled beneath you ... on that plateau ...
    and their campfires ... flickering ... glowing ...
Continue to fly ... toward the outskirts of the city up ahead ...
A city with thick and heavy walls ...
An ancient city with many dirt streets ... with flickering torches
    in the doorways ...
Passing a large building ... you can hear voices and the noise of people
    eating and drinking ...
You can hear laughter ... and singing ...
And it's crowded ... too crowded ...
Continue on ...
Gliding over the furthest city wall ... back to the quiet ...
To the countryside ...

Up ahead ... a ridge of small hills ...
Then coming nearer, you see openings ... the entrances to caves ...
One seems to glow ... lit with a large campfire at the entrance ...
And above ... the star cluster seems to point here ...
As if you were standing directly beneath the tail of the star ...
Rest here a moment ... outside the cave ...

Look around ...
Listen ... hear the muffled sounds of sheep ... bedding down for the night ...
    content ...
Walk through the flock ...

They part quickly ... making a path for you ...
Up ahead ... several men sit and lean close to the opening of the cave ...
Two are bald ... with white beards ...
There are a couple of younger men ...
And three young boys ... just children ...
They all wear soft, warm animal hides ... sandals ...they carry wineskins ...
    and long staffs ...
They turn and look at you ... silently ...
And they smile ... their faces almost glow with wonder ... with joy ...
A wonderful thing has happened ...
God has done something great here ... now ... and you are part of it ...
The shepherds seem proud ... happy ...
And they step back, out of your way ... as if they had been expecting you ...
Is there anything you want to say to them? ...
Anything you want to do? ...

They point toward the entrance of the cave ...
You approach ... slowly ... enter ... and look around ...
There are cows, a few goats, a donkey ...
Everything is hushed ... even the animals ... so satisfied ... so still ...
Beneath you ... there is soft straw to walk on ... dry ... clean ... crisp ...
Step closer ... into the light ...
There are two figures ... resting ... beside the flickering fire ...

You can feel the warmth of the fire on your face ...
A woman holds a bundled baby sleeping quietly ...
The husband looks so proud of his wife and newborn ...
He turns to you ... to welcome you ... to lead you ... to the mother
    and the baby ...
Is there anything you want to say to him? ...
Anything you want to do? ...

The mother leans against a thick pile of straw ...
She holds the child close to her ... cradled in her arms and wrapped in
    tattered strips of cloth ...
Then she looks up into your eyes and smiles ...
She is so very proud ...
She lifts the cover from his face so you can see ...
The baby ... beautiful ... happy ... blinks ... smiles ...
And something deep within you knows that God has been born into
    the world ...
Here ... now ... God has become human ... become just like you ...
God has been born ... a new baby ...

The light from the fire seems to make his face glow ... so bright ...
Then the mother invites you to come closer ...
She raises her arms ... offering the child to you ...
She slides the new born baby into your waiting arms ...
You can feel the warmth ... the softness ... the movement of gentle new life ...
Life ...
The life of God ... in your arms ... fragile and alive ... and so real ...
Is there anything you want to say? ...
Anything you would like to do? ...

And the mother explains that she has been asked ... by God ... to take care
    of Jesus ...
She is to care for him ... until he is old enough to be given to the world ...
To protect him ... nurture him ... and to love him ...
But she needs your help ...
Can you? ... Can you help care for this child of God? ...
Can you help God to grow ... caring for him with love? ...
Is there anything you would like to say? ...
Anything you would like to do? ...

Mary gently ... carefully ... takes the baby back into her arms ...
She tells you that you also have God ... within you ...
And God must grow there too ...
Your task is to bring God to the world as well ...
And she can help you with that ...

Mary asks if God can use your hands to help others ...
She takes your hands ... kisses them softly ... making your hands holy ...
Then she asks if God can use your ears to hear the cry of others ...
Then she gently kisses your ears ... anointing them ...
She asks if God can use your heart to love others ...
And she softly touches your heart with her kiss to consecrate your heart
    to God ...
She hugs you in her arms with the infant baby ...
And thanks you ...

She nods to you ... and you now know ... that within you ... rests Jesus ...
Ready to grow ...
Ready to use your hands ...
To use your ears ...
And to love others with your heart ... Christ's heart ...

Be at peace …
Know that God will always remain within you …
And will never leave …
God will always love others through you …
Know how sacred you are …
Feel the loving heart of God within you …
And be at peace …
And rest …

Think of all you've seen …
All you've heard …
And all you've felt …
And know that God is ready within you …
In your hands, your arms, your heart …
And you can bring him to others so they will know God too …
He is within …
Within …

When you're ready to leave Israel … and come back here …
Know that God is still with you … and will never leave …
You are not alone …
There are so many people who need you …
And need God …
Now come back here …
And be at peace …
When you're ready you may slowly open your eyes …
And I would ask you not to talk to others or distract them …
Just quietly think about what you've just experienced …
And be at peace …
Peace.

Meditation Two

Jesus the Teen-ager

The dreams and aspirations of our youth are given new life as God renews his will for us. Significant people from our lives meet us in this meditation, sharing their gifts and talents, and providing us with abilities that will be necessary for our future success. Inspired by Luke 2:41-50. The use of relaxation technique four is suggested. Time: 12 minutes

And we pray:
Lord Jesus Christ …
We come to you in meditation …
To discover who we are and the possibilities you offer …
Help us to see with your vision … to see our lives as they can be with
     you standing close …
Remain with us Lord …
Give us strength and hope …
Remain close …
Close.

With your eyes still closed …
Go to your favorite place where you can be alone … and safe …
All alone and very safe …
Look around at the familiar things …
Each bringing to mind a happy memory …
A memory of a time that was good … a time of contentment …
A happy memory when you were young and playful …
When you were curious … when you were free …
Close your eyes tighter … and feel the warmth of those memories …
Feel the warmth of a friendship …
Of someone who cares for and knows you better than you know yourself …
Stand there with your eyes closed and feel a new friend coming up
     behind you …
Know that you are safe and the friend will protect you …
From behind you … feel the warmth of his love … the depth of his caring …
     his gentle playfulness …
From behind … he gently cups his hands over your eyes like a playful
     friend …
He gently laughs and, like a special friend that has missed you …
     he gives you a hug …

He turns you around and you can look up and see the smiling face of a
    teen-ager ... of Jesus ...
Jesus when he was a teen-ager ...
Look at his youthful eyes that sparkle ...
Eyes that look right into you ... deeply ... knowing your joys as well
    as your hurts ...
Eyes that can see beyond any walls you may have built ...
Walls that were to protect ... walls that now melt ...
Melt ...

Look into the gentle eyes of a young Jesus who understands so well ...
    and can see the beauty in you that has been hidden ...
Listen to the Lord thank you for inviting him to be with you ...
He has come to you in your favorite place ... so now he asks to take you to
    his favorite place ...
Where he feels very much at home ...
The Lord takes your hand ... softly slides his hand around yours ...
Firmly but gently he takes your hand ...
And you feel secure ...
He takes you to a building ... a place of worship ... a place of prayer ...
What does the place of worship look like to you? ...
Is it large? ... small? ... bright? ... dim? ...
And he tells you of the time when he met the ancient ones here ...
    men of great wisdom ...
Here is where he discovered who he was ... and found strength to begin
    his destiny ... his task ...
And those teachers shared their gifts with him ... their talents ...
They encouraged him ...
They helped him become free.
And now it's your turn ... and Jesus promises that he will stay close to you ...
    to show you ... to help you ...
Is there anything you want to say to Jesus? ...
Anything you want to do? ...
Be at peace ...

Jesus now stands before you ... smiling with contentment ...
Standing before you ... he quietly asks you to close your eyes ...
He raises his hands and softly places his fingers over your closed eyelids ...
    gently rubbing them as if he were pushing away the pressure ...
    the tension ...
He tells you that you are free ... there will be no more expectations ...
    no more demands ... no more pressure ...

34

Just be who you are ... and be loved as you are ... without all the
   expectations ...
Nothing is required ... nothing is called for ...
And you can feel the miraculous touch of Jesus and he seems to rub away
   the darkness from your closed eyes ...
You can see yourself years from now ... in a new way ...
Fulfilling God's will ... fulfilling God's plan ...
Becoming the person you dream of ... the person that God hopes you will
   be someday ...
Be at peace ... and be filled with delight ...
With your eyes closed ... how do you see yourself? ...
What is that person like ... the you that is yet to come? ...
Is there anything you would like to ask that person? ...
Anything you would like to say? ...
Be at peace ...

Jesus wipes the dream from your eyes ... and he asks if he can invite some
   people to join you ...
With your eyes still closed ... see the smile in the Lord's eyes ...
Jesus calls out the name of that person who is about your own age that you
   admire so much ... the one you wish you could be like ...
And now they stand there ... Jesus and the person you always looked up to
   and admired ... the person you watched closely and even studied ...
The person that has a gift or a talent you wish were yours ...
And they offer you that same gift ... that talent ... that quality ...
They hand to you some of that same gift from themselves ...
And the Lord takes it and presses it into you ...
Listen to the Lord explain to you how you can use this ability to fulfill
   God's will ...
Listen carefully ...
How is it part of the dream you wish for? ...

The Lord now calls out the name of the adult who has had the greatest effect
   on your life so far ...
Of all the adults in your neighborhood or at school or where you work ...
   the adult you have let affect your life ... and change it ...
They come to you and smile ...
They remind you of that special gift they already know you have ... a talent ...
   an ability that you can share with others ...
A gift you have that you can be proud of ... maybe it is not fully
   developed yet ... maybe you don't use it all the time ...

But it is a gift you have begun to use …
And they are proud of you …
They give you a hug …
Is there anything you want to say to this adult? …
Anything you would like to do? …

And now they take part of their own best gift … their finest ability …
    that quality you most admire in them …
And they hand part of that gift to you … like a seed …
The Lord takes that gift-seed and presses it into you … so it will grow
    strong and develop …
A gift from them to you …
Listen to the Lord as he explains how to help this gift to grow … to make
    you stronger and better …
How can this new gift help you and be a benefit? …
The Lord explains how you can use this new gift to help bring about
    the Father's will …
Listen to the Lord … be still and listen …

The Lord now calls out the name of the person in your family that you
    admire the most …
Of all the people in your family … cousins … aunts … uncles … grandparents
    … those that are near or those that are far …
Those that are living or those that can only be with you from heaven …
The Lord now calls out the name of the person in your family that you
    admire the most …
The one you wish you could be like …
And now they are standing there before you with the Lord …
They are so pleased with you …
They come to you and brush the hair from your forehead and give you
    a big hug …
And they feel so warm and loving … you can feel their goodness …
They look at you now and with keen wisdom tell you one of your
    best qualities … something they see in you that most people have
    not yet seen …
And they explain how this gift you already have can be developed …
    and can grow …

Now tell them the one quality you love about them the most …
    that special something that makes them special in your heart …
    that ability you wish you had as well …
And they smile and then take some of that gift like a seed and offer it to you …

And the Lord takes the seedling of that gift and he presses it into you ...
with love and with patience ... and you can feel it starting to grow ...
gently ... slowly ...
Listen now as the Lord explains how you can use this new gift to help bring
about the Father's will ...
Listen to the Lord ... be still and listen ...

Now Jesus steps behind you and again places his fingers up to your eyes ...
gently rubs ... and asks you to look at yourself ...
Look into the future to see the you that you can become ... the you that God
has created you to become ... the you that will fulfill God's plan for you ...
And Jesus explains how the gifts of all those special people will help you to
become the person you dream of becoming ... the person God hopes
you will be ...
You can see in yourself the gift from the person your
own age that you admire the most ...
And the gift from the adult that has affected you the most ...
And from the person in your family that you admire the most ...
Each of the gifts ... so very important ...
Be at peace and be proud of your possibilities ...

In joy ... Jesus gives you a big hug ...
Is there anything you want to say to him? ...
Anything you would like to do? ...

Jesus promises he will be with you always to help you develop those
gifts and to help you learn to use them ...
He promises to never force himself on you ...
But he will always be standing near you ... waiting for you to ask for
his help ...
And if you ask him ... he promises to help you to fulfill that dream ...
to become all that God has created you to be ...
Be at peace ...
Know that the Lord is so near to you ...
Ready to help if only you ask ...
Be at peace ...

When you are ready, take stock of your gifts ... remember each of the abilities
that were given to you ...
And bring them with you ...

Come back to this room … and be at peace … and when you are ready …
   you may open your eyes … but don't look at anyone or try to get their
   attention …
Just think of all the gifts you have been given …
And know that the Lord will help you to grow …
And be at peace …
At peace.

Meditation Three

Baptism by John

We discover a new commitment to God while joining with our community of
fellow believers in an act of repentance in the Jordan River. Inspired by
Matthew 3:1-6. The use of relaxation technique three is suggested.
Time: 12 minutes

And we pray:
Lord Jesus Christ ...
Guide us as we meditate ...
Give us your Spirit ... to direct us and lead us closer to you ...
Help us to find our need for you ... deep within ...
And to hunger for you ...
So be with us Lord ...
Guide us in peace ...
Stay near ...
Be near ...

With your eyes still closed ...
Travel beyond the barren deserts of ancient Israel ...
Beyond the bleached sand of Israel's desert ...
You can feel the dry air ... parched air ...
Almost burning as you breathe ...
The glaring sun ... throbbing its heat on your face ... robbing you of shade ...
Roasting you ... baking you ...

Keep moving over the desert that shimmers with heat ...
You are approaching a string of palm trees up ahead ... along a river ...
A cluster of lush green ... soaking up the coolness of the narrow,
    gentle river ...
The Jordan River ...
A long flowing oasis ... snaking in and out ... across the desert ...
And here it is cool ... and calm ... and peaceful ...

Look ... carefully ... a stream of people are gathering ...
From all directions ...
Gathering at the river's edge ...
Gathering to be refreshed ... at the cool water's edge ...

And a man stands in the stream ...
A man dressed with a hide of camel's hair ... a leather strap wrapped tightly
    around his waist ...
He looks wild ... his hair long and snarled ...
His eyes filled with a kind of fire ... and wild exuberance ...
Like a mad lover ... obsessed ... wanting to tell the world of his love ...
His love of God ...

And he calls out ... to those who gather ...
He cries out ... he invites ... he gathers ...
And the people cluster at the river's edge to hear him ...
They listen ... intently ... they ponder ... they nod their heads ...
    or shake them ...
The man speaks a word that seems to come from God ...
God whispers through the words of the baptizer ...
God calls and gathers ...

Rest at the water's edge ... and listen ...
Listen to the word from God that the baptizer speaks ...
Hear God tell you about this time which has come ... now ...
A time for a new beginning ...
God's promise of harmony and understanding ... of inner peace ...

God promises that a time is at hand when he will walk with those who
    love him ... together ...
He promises them an entire new world ...
And God promises to be their joy ... their laughter ... their happiness ...
And all of your tears and sadness could be ended ...
And you could be part of that ... if you choose ... if you want ...

And he tells you that only sin has kept you away ...
That only sin has prevented you from seeing God ...
From recognizing the new world ...
Sin keeps you blind to God ...
Only sin has separated you ... kept you from this incredible new beginning ...
Those mistakes we've made that blind us ...
Blind us to new life with God ...
Blind us to God ...

What has separated you from God ... blinded you from recognizing God ...
    and his possibilities in your life? ...
What mistakes have kept God away? ... what regrets? ... what hurts? ...
What mistakes have been made? ...

What could have been changed? ...
What would God have wanted to be different? ...
Sin has hurt ... has hurt you so deeply ...
And that sin has hurt someone else ...
But be at peace because the hurt can be healed ... that sin reconciled ...
     forgiven ...

What would you like to be healed? ...
What do you need forgiven ... forgotten by God ... brought to an end? ...

The baptizer invites you to begin again ... with new sight ... clear sight ...
     God's sight ...
Without the guilt of yesterday ...
To begin again ...
To become ready for the new world ...
To be healed from the mistake ...

And God can do it if you are ready ...
Prepared by John ...
Washed by this prophet sent by God ...
Are you willing to take the step into the water? ...
To be washed clean? ...
To meet God in healing? ...

And the baptizer comes to you ... gently holds out his hand ...
He invites you to come ... enter the water ...
Be refreshed ... become clean ... forgiven and healed ...
By God ...
Who can touch you ... and heal you ...
To be made ready for something even greater than ever before ...
Is there anything you want to say to the baptizer? ...
Anything you want to do? ...

And in the heat of the day ...
The baptizer slowly walks with you ... into the water ...
And you can feel the coolness ... of the water at your feet ...
Cool but not cold ... refreshing ...
A few more steps into the slowly rambling waters ...
You step further ... so the water rises to your knees ...
You can feel the safety of the baptizer's strong arm ...
His strong arm holding you ... protecting you ... guiding you safely ...
No harm will come to you ...

You feel the safety of God's love …
Is there anything you want to say to him? …
Anything you want to do? …

And the baptizer cups the refreshing water into his hands …
     and slowly pours it over you …
Washing you … purifying you … preparing you …
Making you ready for the hand of God's healing …
Ready for God to come to you …

And you can feel the Spirit of God's love come over you …
Leaving a mark of love on you … for God …
With your eyes closed … feel the peace of God …
Like a wave of peace that falls over you … slowly … gently …
     covering you …
Be at peace …

The baptizer gently holds your lowered face … raises you up …
Your eyes meet …
And he smiles …
He welcomes you …
With pride …

And suddenly you notice that the face of the baptizer takes a new shape …
     changes …
His face becomes soft … filled with gentle love … almost glows …
His face becomes transformed and you recognize the face of Jesus …
Smiling … forgiving … understanding … in love with you …
He holds your beautiful face gently in his hands …
Your eyes meet …
And quietly … he tells you how proud he is of you …
How much he loves you …
And be at peace … as he wraps his arms around you … holds you close
     in his arms …

His arms are firm … but gentle …
And the Lord asks you to put your trust in him …
You know how safe it is …
And the Lord tells you he will protect you …
You are safe … with him …

He looks into your eyes … as if he sees beyond them … deep into you …
     recognizing a new person about to emerge …

He looks with understanding ... with compassion ... with forgiveness ...
And he asks ... what can he forgive? ...
What do you want him to wash away? ...
He turns his face toward you ... his ear close to you ... to hear you whisper ...
And quietly ... speak to the Lord ... tell him the mistake ... the sin ...
    that needs to be forgiven ...
He slides his gentle arm over your shoulders ...
He asks ... he whispers ... what can he do to make it better? ...
    to help you in the future ...
What can he do to make it change and never happen again? ...
And be at peace ...
For the Lord understands ...

And then ... cupping clean, clear water in his sacred hands he slowly pours
    the holy water over you ...
You can feel his Spirit ... the spirit of forgiveness ... the spirit of
    healing, wash over you ...
And you are new ...
Washed ... made pure ... holy ...
And be at peace ...
Peace ...

He gently wraps his arms around you and tells you how much he loves you ...
And he holds you close ... nothing could ever come between you ...
He draws your face against his chest ...
You can hear his heartbeat ...
You have been made new ...
You can start fresh and new again ...
Is there anything you want to say to the Lord? ...
Anything you would like to do? ...

The Lord promises you that he will never abandon you or leave you alone ...
He will be with you always ...
He will never leave you ...
And be at peace ...

When you are ready ... leave the water ... and the desert ...
And return here ...
Knowing that the Lord is still with you to help you ...
And strengthen you ...
Come back ...

And when you are ready … you may open your eyes …
I'd ask you not to talk to anyone or distract them …
But quietly think back about all you have felt and experienced …
And be at peace …
With God's forgiveness …
For you are new.

Meditation Four

Temptation in the Desert

We find that we have the divine gifts of faithfulness and determination, enabling us to triumph over the temptations in our lives. Inspired by Matthew 4:1-11. The use of relaxation technique four is suggested. Time: 11 minutes

And we pray:
Loving God …
We come to you with open hearts as we meditate …
We want to be confident of your love, but sometimes our doubt undermines our total trust …
We pray today that you will deepen our faith so that we may rely on you more completely …
We pray that your kingdom may unfold in our lives …
That your kingdom may become real …
And that we too may be real …

With your eyes still closed …
Take a slow journey …
Travel to a place where you can be all alone …
Where no one else would venture to intrude …
A place where there are no distractions … nothing fancy … a place where you can think … and be still …
With your eyes closed … see the emptiness around you … like a void …
Feel the loneliness …
Know how vulnerable you are … how unprotected … you are alone with nothing else around you …
And now with your eyes closed … look inside yourself and search for some kind of trust …
In your solitude … can you find any kind of trust within you? …
Is there someone you trust in? …
Find the trust if it is there …
What kind of trust is it? …
Who or what have you placed your trust in? …
What will protect you? …

Be aware suddenly that there is someone else nearby and that you are not alone …

45

You look around … but you see no one … you are sure that someone is
near … someone that you can't see … yet you feel you are safe …
So just rest and relax a moment and trust your feelings …

Feel the presence of the other person …
Feel their goodness and gentleness …
Feel the presence of this person's incredible understanding and
forgiveness …
Feel the gentle softness of this love …
This feeling is like drawing near to God …
Know that God is with you … that Jesus is with you … even though you
don't see him …
Know that God is with you in a special way right now …
And rest in this loving presence of God …
Rest and be at peace …
Peace …

And still … even though you can't see the Lord … know that he is near …
Very near …
But in a strange way you are still alone …

Quietly reflect by yourself what your real needs are …
Think about what you really desire for yourself … not for anyone else …
but something that you really crave and have decided that you want
more than anything else …

In this quiet and lonely place … with your imagination … build a scene …
like in a movie … build a scene that represents how or when you are
tempted to satisfy your own inner cravings and desires …
Know that the needs of others will become unimportant …
because your desires are stronger than theirs ….
Know that deep down … you want to have those cravings satisfied …
Imagine what you must do for yourself to satisfy those longings …
to get whatever you are aching for … knowing that no one will ever know
what you are really feeling …
Perhaps it is as if you are controlled by your craving …
By what you ache for …

And now you can feel the Lord … Jesus puts his gentle hand on
your shoulder …
The Lord whispers in your ear …
And he tells you that he understands … he knows … because he is just
as human as you …

And be at peace …
Is there anything you want to say to Jesus? …
Anything you would like to do? …

And now Jesus tells you that he can offer you something better …
    he can offer something more important …
Be still and watch the picture that Jesus draws in your imagination …
    of something better that he can give … something better than what
    you crave …
If you can depend upon the Lord … if you can trust …
Jesus hands you a gift of hope … hope that will keep you strong …
And healthy …
Hope … it is now yours … part of you … forever …
Is there anything you want to say to Jesus? …
Anything you want to do? …

And suddenly you are alone again … in that place of plainness …
And with your eyes closed … look inside yourself and find a time when
    you were unsure …
A time when you were fearful that things wouldn't work out …
That something wouldn't be right …
And with your eyes closed … paint that scene like in a movie …
    so that you stand in that situation again …
Frozen in time so you can see it again … and feel it again …
A time when you wanted to be sure that God would make everything
    perfect, but you had doubts …
You weren't sure …
The doubts were too strong … you were tempted to give up … to despair …
Feel how strong those fears and doubts can be … pressuring you …

But they won't crush you …
Because again you can feel the hand of Jesus on your shoulder …
A quiet and gentle whisper in your ear …
And he asks you to trust … because if you let him … he can do
    wondrous things …
And he stands in the midst of your scene … to show you … to give you
    just a brief glimpse of what could happen … how he would let it develop …
    if he were given the chance …

Then he whispers in your ear how much he loves you and promises that in
    the end … he can have something wonderful happen …
If you can trust … if you can let him be God … if you can have faith …

And then Jesus hands you another gift …
This is a gift of faith to keep you strong …
And to keep you close to God …
Close …
Even in times when you have doubts … or are unsure …
Faith to keep you strong … even when things are beyond your control …
Faith …
Is there anything you would like to say to the Lord? …
Anything you would like to do? …
Be at peace …

Once more … return to that place of plainness where you are alone …
    with no distractions …
Alone …
And with your eyes closed look inside yourself and find a feeling of
    weakness …
That sense of being inadequate and not capable …
That feeling you would never want anyone else to see …
And if you could mask … or hide it … you would cover it with power …
Just feel the need for power so that no one can ever see the weakness in you …
Feel how secure you would be with that incredible power …
But what kind of power would you need? …
Power over others? … Power to do without the support and approval
    of others? … Power to get others' attention? … Power to control? …
Feel that power and what you could do with it …
Paint a scene like in a movie where you can watch yourself with all
    that power …
How does it feel? …

Once again … you can feel the Lord's hand on your shoulder …
    that familiar whisper in your ear … the quiet and gentle voice of God
    that can bring your scene to its later stages …
And the Lord shows you how power can ultimately hurt and control others
    so they are no longer free and able to love …
And the possible darkness of power …
Power …

But Jesus wipes it away and whispers …
Listen to the Lord tell you how God glories in weakness …
    how admitting your weakness is good and makes you more human …
How you can be more gentle …
How weakness is not threatening to others but invites them to be closer …

48

And how weakness and love work together to help each other ...
    to make our love strong ...
To make God strong ... and it becomes your strength ...
    love can be your strength ...
Loving strength ...
And the Lord hands you another gift ... a gift of love ...
Squeeze that gift of love deeply to yourself so that it can become
    part of you ...
And you can feel the strength of that divine love from God ...
And be at peace ...

Know that you are filled with the gifts of God ...
His gift of hope ... his gift of faith ... and his incredible gift of love ...
    and feel the divine strength radiating from within you ...
Giving you courage and giving you hope ...
Is there anything you would like to say to the Lord? ...
Anything you would like to do? ...

Jesus promises you that he will always be with you ... he will never
    leave you ... even if you can't see him ... even if you can't feel him ...
Always with you ...
And be at peace ...
Peace ...

Filled with faith, hope, and love from God ... slowly return here ...
    still filled with the gifts from God ...
When you are ready you may open your eyes and quietly reflect on all that
    you saw and felt ... all that you have just experienced ...
And know the gifts God has given to you ...
And be at peace ...
Peace.

The Call of the First Disciples

Like the first disciples, we too learn that we have been called to learn from and follow Christ. Inspired by Luke 5:1-11. The use of relaxation technique one is suggested. Time: 14 minutes

And we pray:
Loving Father in heaven …
You call each of us … your chosen …
You call us by name to follow Christ as his disciples …
As we meditate today, guide us with your Holy Spirit to know your call
     from Jesus …
To discover our roots of faith and the mission you invite us to undertake …
That we may become closer to you…
That we may work together with you …

With your eyes still closed …
Think of that place where you first remember hearing about God …
Maybe it was when you were a child …
Maybe when you were a little older … maybe it wasn't that long ago …
Where were you when you first heard about God? …
Were you at home? … in church? … in school? … with a friend? …
When do you first remember thinking about God? …
Where were you? …
With your eyes still closed …
Take a journey to that place … where you can now be all alone …
     no one else to distract you …
A place that is safe … where you can now feel comfortable …
     and be all alone …

Look around you and see the different things …
Familiar things you had forgotten about …
Personal things that are still there as they were then …
Is it bright there? … dark? …
Maybe warm? … cool? …
Are there any familiar smells? …
Can you hear the echoes of the past? …
What were some of those sounds from long ago? …

Now … try to remember what sparked your attention about God at
    that time …
Can you overhear someone talking about God? …
Maybe someone was explaining something to you …
Sharing something they believed with you …
Are they actually there? … or on the radio? … or television? …
Where is the voice that you hear? …
Listen carefully and hear the tone in the voice … why are they saying this?…
    why are they talking about God? …
How do you feel when you first hear them? …
What are you thinking of? …
What is it they are saying? …
How does it effect you? …
And be at peace …
Peace …

And now … you can hear the sound of the person's name …
A voice is calling to them …
A voice that invites them to be near you …
And they now stand there with you …
Face to face …
Just the two of you …
You and the person you first remember telling you about God …
Ask them why they were willing to share … to say what they did …
    to talk about God … to talk about their faith …
Listen to them quietly explain …

Ask them how following God has affected their life …
    what was most important? … how did God influence them? …
Is there anything you would like to say to that person? …
Anything you would like to do? …
And be at peace …
Peace.

Look inside yourself now … and see the faith that you have …
Your need for God … your belief in God … your trust in God …
But where did that faith come from? …
When did you first realize you had that faith? …
When did you first know that God could help you? …
When did you first realize that God was there for you? …

With your eyes closed … travel to that place where you first realized
    you had faith … that you knew God was there for you …

that there was a God you could depend on ...
Were you young? ... a teen-ager? ... alone? ... with others? ...
What was the situation? ... Where did you realize this faith? ...
Travel to this place ...
Let it be frozen in time ... so you can move around invisibly and see
    the situation ...
What kind of place was it where you first discovered your faith? ...
    is it inside? ... outside? ... is it dark? ... or bright? ...
Are you alone? ... or with others? ...
What is happening? ...
What did you need? ... or want? ...
How could God have helped you at this time? ...
Was there someone there who was part of that situation? ...
What did they do? ... Why were they there? ... How were they part
    of your realization of your faith? ...
And be at peace ...
Peace ...

And now if you listen carefully in the silence .... you can hear a voice ...
    a name being called ...
Listen carefully and you can hear the name of the person who was part of
    your first experience of God ...
A gentle voice that calls them to be near you ...
An invitation from God to be with you ... softly ... gently ...
They stand in front of you now ...
And you can feel a new kind of understanding coming from them ...
    a kind of peace ... as if God were with them ...
With courage ... explain how you discovered your need for God ...
    tell them when you first realized that God could help you and be there
    for you ... when you first needed God ...

And they listen with love ... and they nod and understand ...
    and smile because they too have felt that ...
And they give you a big hug ...
And you can feel their joy ... and their peace ...
And it becomes part of you ...
At peace ...
Peace ...
Is there anything you want to say to them? ...
Anything you want to do? ...

And with your eyes closed again …

Look deep inside yourself … and see all the things that have happened to you
    over the past few years … like a movie going by …

And look for the most recent time when you thought about God …
    when you needed God to help you … or to protect you … or a time
    when you really felt that God was near … doing something for you …

Where were you when you last felt close to God? … with others perhaps? …
    maybe alone? …

And with your eyes closed … travel to that place where you most recently
    felt close to God … and look around to see the situation …

What were you thinking about? … How did you feel? … and be confident
    that God was with you …

Very close … with you …

What did God do? …

How did you know that God was with you? …

Who was there … part of that situation … who caused it or who was
    just there …. or who was it about? …

And be at peace …

Peace.

Now … be still … listen … listen carefully …

With your ears … listen …

And hear the silence … alone … quiet …

And again listen … but with your heart instead of your ears … as if closing
    your ears and opening your heart to hear new and different things …

Focus on your heart and its ability to hear in new ways …

And listen to feelings … deep inside … with your heart …

And with the feelings of your heart … hear the voice … the quiet voice
    of God … who slowly says your name …

Slowly … gently … hushed … God pronounces your name …
    as if calling you with love …

God calls to you and whispers your name into your heart …

And waits … waits for you to reply …

No one else …

He calls again and waits for you …

With a special love and devotion … God calls to you …

And as you hear your name … or think about God … you suddenly feel that
    you are no longer alone …

Don't turn around … don't look about you … just feel the other person's
    presence …

Someone who is loving ... and never judges ...
Someone you can trust and feel very comfortable with ...
And now you can feel the warmth of his love near you ... feel his presence ...
And now he takes your hand ... standing next to you ... together ...
And you know that he has been there all the time ... even when you
    weren't aware of it ...
You can look now and see the gentle face of Jesus ... full of admiration
    for you ...
And listen to him ...
Jesus asks what you would do for him ... if you were given more faith ...
How would you hand on that faith ... share it with others? ...

And the Lord gently wraps his arms around you to hug you and you
    feel a growing strength ... you feel the power of his faith becoming
    part of you ...
Silently you feel his confidence pass to you ... the courage ... the strength
    to depend upon God ... new faith ... stronger faith ...
And the Lord's faith fills you ... helping you to become his disciple ...
    his follower ...
And the Lord asks you ... with your power and faith ... to continue his
    mission ...
He asks you to continue his work ... to bring his love and healing to those
    around you ... those who do not have strong faith like you ...
Is there anything you would like to say to the Lord? ...
Anything you would like to ask? ...
And be at peace ...

The Lord promises that he will be with you ... always ...
Always ...
The Lord promises that he will always guide you if you will trust ...
    always help you if you will be confident in him ... if you will use the
    new faith he has given to you ...
He will quietly speak to your heart if you listen carefully with that gift of
    faith ... a gift to keep you close ... to help you be strong ...
    to be his disciple ...
You will never have to be afraid ... or worry ...
He will be with you always ... even if you can't see him ... even if you can't
    feel him ... he promises to be with you ... always ...
And be at peace ...
Peace ...

When you are ready ... I would like you to come back here ...

Know that you are not alone ... and that you bring back with you the
      renewed faith ... the power and the strength given to you by God ...
      so that you may be his disciple ... and continue his mission ...

You may open your eyes ... but don't look at anyone or try to get
      anyone's attention ...

Just silently think about all that you have just experienced ...
      all you have seen ... all you have thought about ...

What you thought of the first time you heard about God ... the people
      and the place ... and the first time you felt God near you and how you
      depended upon him ... and the most recent time you experienced the
      feeling of God helping you ... and all those people that were there for you ...
      and brought you God's love and healing ...

And just reflect on how your faith has grown ...

And know that God's faith is part of you ... a gift from God to continue his
      mission ... his work ... his healing ... and now it is all yours ...

And be at peace ...

Peace.

Meditation Six

Rejection at Nazareth

Finding new strength through Christ's power to accept others even in the midst of their rejection of him, we learn to accept and forgive those who have rejected us. Inspired by Luke 4:16-30. The use of relaxation technique three is suggested. Time: 12 minutes

And we pray:
Almighty God …
You sent your son Jesus …
To gather us, your people, into your kingdom, into your new family …
Yet he was met with the pain of rejection and disappointment …
We too have known those same rejections and disappointments …
The hurts that you alone desire to heal …
As we meditate today … send us your healing Spirit … guide us, so that we
    may come to know the strength in your love and acceptance …
To know your love …
To know your acceptance …
To know you …

With your eyes still closed …
Feel yourself going to a place of grayness …
A place that is neither dark nor light …
Neither warm nor cool …
Where there is nothing around you …
Where you can be alone and safe …
Nothing to harm you …
Or distract you …
Safe …

But you are not alone …
With your eyes closed, feel the comforting arm of our Lord near you …
Wrapped around you …
Protecting you …
Safe …

Jesus wants to share something very important with you …
He takes your hand …

And together you travel quickly to the ancient town of Nazareth …
The town where Jesus grew up as a boy …
You feel the heat of Nazareth … the dry air …
You can taste the dry dust of the town's streets …
The day is bright …

Standing in the city street … holding the hand of Jesus … you can see many
    people quickly walking past you toward the corner …
And then around the corner …
Their robes billow … flutter from walking so fast …
They rush … they don't want to be late …
Together you and Jesus join the crowd …
Around the corner … to the building at the end …
The building with crisscross screens that shield the doors and windows
    from the heat of the sun …
And the people enter …
This place of worship … this synagogue …
Together … you and the Lord … go inside …
But they don't see you … they only see the Lord …
You've become his invisible friend … to watch … to experience …
    to share … invisibly …

Slowly look around the large rectangular room …
The cool stone walls … the strong columns with intricate designs …
    stone seats along the walls …
Everyone is sitting cross-legged on little carpets on the floor … all facing
    the platform with the canopy and the hanging lamps …
Two men on the platform with thick, long beards extend the large scroll
    to Jesus as if asking him to read …
Jesus takes you by the hand … walks with you through the gathered crowd …
Together you both ascend to the platform … but no one can see you …
    they see only Jesus …

Look around at the faces of the crowd … how they all watch … and wait …
    in anticipation …
Look at the expressions on their faces … some are bored … some curious …
    some eager …
Turn to Jesus … and listen …
He unrolls the scroll and begins to read … he teaches …
Listen to Jesus as he teaches them … see his power … his enthusiasm …
    his courage … his determination …
And yet the gentleness … the peaceful compassion in his voice …

58

Again look out at the crowd ... look at their faces ... as they focus their
    attention on the Lord ...
How their expressions slowly change ... strangely change to anger
    and bitterness ...
Look at the faces of the people ... their eyebrows knot up ...
    pinch together ... glare ...
Jesus tells them that he has been sent to bring God's love to all people ...
    not just these people of his own hometown ...
But they want God's power exclusively for themselves ...

They want Jesus to be their own magician ... to fulfill only their demands...
    they are possessive and demanding ... they are jealous ...
    they refuse to let Jesus be free ...
And listen to Jesus plead that he must obey God's desire ... not theirs ...
Jesus wants to give himself to others ... to bring love even to their enemies,
    who need him as well ...
And the people get angry ... because Jesus won't allow himself to be
    controlled by them ...
They become belligerent ... they don't want any part of him ...
They grumble against the Lord ... and threaten to get even ... to take back
    their faith ...
They leave him and walk away ... several turn back and shake their fist in
    the air at him ... yell at him ... that they want no part of him ...
And they leave Jesus ... alone ...
Deserted ... rejected ... Jesus sits alone ...
And you are there ... next to him ...
Feel his loneliness ... his hurt ... his suffering ... try to feel the rejection
    he feels ...
Wanting to love ... but not being accepted ...
Wanting to give of himself ... but being denied ...
Is there anything you want to say to Jesus? ...
Anything you want to do? ...

Now share with Jesus about a time when you also were rejected ...
    when people said cruel things ... or when someone said they
    didn't need you ... and left you ... alone ...
Explain to Jesus how you felt ... maybe alone ... maybe hurt ...
    disappointed ... confused ... maybe rejected ...

Explain to the Lord your feelings of rejection ...
Did those negative feelings hold you prisoner? ...

Did you feel like you couldn't do your best? …
Did the feelings of rejection hold you back? …

Watch the expression of understanding on the face of the Lord as he nods …
And Jesus puts his arms around you and says that he knows how you felt …
It hurts …
It's like a dark cloud that settles on you to hold you back …
He knows … He has felt the same pain as yours …

And then Jesus gently calls out the name of the person that has rejected
    you the most …
The person that has turned their back to you …
Ignored you …
Left you …
And suddenly that person is standing there …
You … the Lord … and the person that hurt you by rejecting you …

Jesus takes you to them … waves his hand in front of them so that you
    can see the thoughts and feelings of that person who has rejected you …
You can see their loneliness …
All the scars left from their disappointments …
And their own suffering …
Then Jesus points out to you their feelings of regret …
Their feelings of loneliness …
They just don't know how to let you be free …
To be who you really are instead of who they would rather have you be …
Who they want you to be …

 But their rejection still hurts …
And Jesus turns to you …
Draws you into his arms …
Holds you …
And you know that the Lord cares … cares deeply for you …
And asks if he can help …
Is there anything you would like to ask Jesus for? …
Anything you would like to say? …

Then Jesus puts his hands into your hands …
And you can feel the strength in his hands …
A power from the Lord's hands comes into yours …
Like you have never felt before … a strength … a determination …
A power from Christ that will help you to do what you know is right …
To hold strong to your beliefs and convictions …

A power to accept someone else in their weakness and confusion ...
    to accept someone else even if they turn from you ...
The power of Christ's love ...
The Lord's love for you ...
Is there anything you want to say to Jesus? ...
Anything you would like to do? ...

Jesus smiles at you with confidence ... approval ...
He points you toward the person who had rejected you ...
Jesus asks you to be patient ...
And to use the new strength he has given you ...
To find the Lord's power to be strong ... deep within you ... strong enough
    to accept that person who hurt you ...
To help that other person by accepting them ... forgiving them ...
    allowing them to make mistakes ...
Is there anything you want to say to them? ...
Anything you can do for them? ...
And be at peace ...

And suddenly that person is gone and you remain alone with Jesus ...
You and Christ ... alone together ...
And he promises that his strength will always be with you ...
If you only ask for it ...
Strength that can protect you and give you comfort ... give you confidence ...
    give you the power to accept others even if they hurt you ...
Because that's when they need your patience ... and your acceptance ...
    and your love ...
You have that gift ... that connection with God ... like a bridge ...
    a power cord that keeps Jesus close to you ...
His ability and gift to accept others unconditionally is now yours ...
Jesus promises that he will never turn from you ...
That he loves you too much to turn away ... no matter what ...
    he will be with you always ...
He will continue to teach you to accept others and to love them ...
Even now you can heal these hurting people with this new power ...
    power from Jesus ...

Jesus holds you close in his arms ...
And you know that he will protect you ... and care for you ...
Always ...
Is there anything you would like to say to the Lord? ...
Is there anything you would like to do? ...

Be at peace ... know that Jesus will never let go of you ... never ...
Know that you still have that powerful strength from the Lord ...
    that it can never be taken from you ...
Power to accept ... power to hold firm ... power from the stronger faith that
    God has given to you ...
And be at peace ...
Peace ...

When you're ready ... come back ... and know that you're not alone ...
There are others here who need from you that gift of acceptance ...
That gift you now have ...
You may open your eyes ...
And be at peace ...
Peace.

Christ's Proclamation of Freedom

Discovering Jesus' call to freedom, we learn that we are called to freedom from unreasonable expectations, freedom from peer pressure, and freedom from fear and anxiety. Inspired by Luke 4:16-19. The use of relaxation technique four is suggested. Time 12 minutes

And we pray:
Almighty God and Father …
Like your son Jesus Christ …
We are totally dependent upon you …
You gave him the freedom necessary to fulfill your will …
The freedom to know your joy and your peace …
And you gave him your Holy Spirit … who is the source of all freedom …
We pray today for your Spirit …
Your Spirit that gives freedom …
We pray that we might trust your Spirit …
As it guides and directs us this day …
In prayer for a new freedom …
Bonded with Christ …
In prayer with you …

With your eyes still closed …
Go to a place where you can be alone …
Where nothing can harm you …
Alone …
Where the light is dim …
A place that is dark …
And it's hard to see …
Where there is only a faint glow …
But still … you feel very safe … nothing can harm you …

And as you look around yourself … you feel a kind of restraint …
    a difficulty in moving …
As if something were weighing you down … holding you back …
    preventing you from reaching great lengths …
But don't fight the feeling … don't fight the restrictions …
Just relax and accept the restraint … the invisible restraint …
It is safe … and nothing will harm you …

Just be aware of something that holds you back …
And be at peace …
Peace …

And then … in your darkness … you also feel a warmth … a kind of
    gentleness drawing near you …
Like the warmth of friendship … and caring … someone who would never
    let anything harmful happen to you …
And you realize that you are not alone …
Beside you stands another person …
One who knows you … and understands you …
Someone you can easily trust …
And in the darkness … with your eyes closed you can feel his loving hands
    softly grasp your shoulders …
Firmly but gently …
Strong and supportive …
And with your eyes still closed … you can make out the gentle face of Jesus
    standing before you …
Whose presence seems to bring incredible comfort …
Incredible peace …
Peace …

The Lord looks down at your hands …
Takes them both in his … like a prayer …
And holds them together firmly … as if to protect them …
You can feel a kind of energy in his hands …
An energy that has great power …
And he begins to trace a symbol in the palm of your hand …
Slowly and carefully … he draws something with the tip of his finger …
In the palm of your hand …
And slowly … quietly … in a whisper … he tells you that the
    Spirit of the Lord is upon him …
And that he has the full power of the Spirit … to share with you …
With power to bring freedom … to you …
Freedom …

And he continues to trace a symbol in the palm of your hand …
A symbol of his power …
One that seems to have a kind of energy …
And strangely … you can feel it pulling at something within you …
    pulling at whatever worry or anxiety it finds within you …
    pulling that worry from you …

64

You can feel that anxiety or worry melt …
Slowly dissolve and vanish …
So that all that remains is trust … trust in Jesus …
For he wants to make you free …
If you will let him …

Jesus quietly tells you that he has great things in store for you …
He has great plans for you …
That together … you can do incredible things …
But as you try to move … you can still feel the heavy weight of something
    holding you back … things that weigh you down …
Jesus promises that this can change … only trust him …

Jesus asks you to focus on your family …
How does your family hold you back? …
How does your family … or someone in your family … take away your
    happiness … keep you from growing? …
Perhaps someone puts too many expectations on you? …
Who in your family holds you back? …

Then Jesus calls out their name … softly … gently …
And suddenly they are with you … Jesus, the person from your family
    that holds you back, and yourself …
Jesus invites you to look inside them … to understand them …
You can see a part of them that is a weakness … a flaw …
Something that even they know is a shortcoming in themselves …
    that they would never admit …that they try to hide …
Or they try to find it in you … so they don't have to acknowledge it
    in themselves …
It's easier to point it out in you … to see it as your flaw …
    but it's really theirs …
And sometimes that hurts …
But Jesus promises you that you can be free of that too …
If only … if only you can first give them freedom … by accepting that flaw
    in them …
To forgive the hurt that the flaw has caused you …
To still love them with their flaw … their weakness …

Jesus smiles because he knows your great potential and he has
    confidence in you …
He begins to trace something in the palm of your hand …
Tracing it with his finger … using the power of his Spirit …

Pressing that Spirit of his ... and its power ... so softly into the palm
of your hand ...
The power of acceptance ... the power to love this person in your family
in spite of their flaw ...
And you can feel a new strength ... from the Lord's gift of his Spirit ...
Strength to forgive and accept them ... to forget the flaw in the person
from your family ... to let them know their flaw is alright ...
and that you can ignore it in them ...
Now standing before you is this person ... with the Lord at your side ...
is there anything you want to say to this person from your family? ...
Is there anything you would like to do? ...

The Lord tells you how proud he is of you ...
The darkness that you have been standing in seems to gain a
little brightness ...
And you seem less restricted ... but still it's difficult to move ...

Then Jesus asks you who it may be at school (or where you work) that seems to
restrain you ... to hold you back from becoming all that you can be ...
Another student or teacher (or employee or supervisor) that may not be
giving you enough credit ... or has the wrong impression of you ...
Someone you have struggled with ...

Jesus calls out their name ... softly ... gently ...
Suddenly they are with you ... Jesus ... the person from school
(or where you work) ... and yourself ...
And Jesus invites you to see them as he does ... to see even their short-
comings... their flaws ... their weaknesses ...
But Jesus explains that he can still accept them ... he can still be patient
with them ... until they are able to correct their own flaw ...
until they are free enough to accept themselves ...
Because they too need freedom to work on their own weakness ...
Instead of trying to hide it or point it out in others ...
They need the acceptance that only your forgiveness can bring ...

And again he traces something in the palm of your hand ...
A word ... for you ...
Tracing it with his finger ... using the power of his Spirit ...
Pressing that Spirit of his ... and its power ... softly into the palm of
your hand ...
The power of acceptance ... the power to love this person in spite of
their flaw ...

And you can feel more strength ... from the Lord's gift of his Spirit ...
Strength to forgive and accept ... the flaw in the person from school
    (or work) ...
And now ... while you stand before this person ... with the Lord at your
    side ... is there anything you want to say to this person from
    school (or work)? ...
Is there anything they need to hear from you? ...
Anything you need to do? ...

The Lord tells you how proud he is of you ...
And be at peace ...

It seems to be getting brighter ...
And with a deeper strength ... you feel a new flexibility ...
Jesus takes your hands again ...
Folds them together ... and then gently opens them up revealing
    an image of yourself ... like in a mirror ...
You are able to look more closely at yourself ...
Standing apart from yourself ... but intimately close ... you can see
    your feelings ... your thoughts ...
Jesus touches your eyes in a special way ... so that you can see yourself
    as God sees you ...
You can see the joys ... and the sadness ... the disappointments
    and the surprises ...
You can even see your strengths and your fears ...

Jesus faces you ... holds your hands together in his ...
And asks you to look at yourself ... to see the way you may be holding
    yourself back from being everything God has created you to be ...
What is it that causes your doubts or your insecurities? ...
What takes away your confidence? ...
How do you make yourself a prisoner of weakness and darkness? ...

Again ... Jesus begins to trace a word in the palm of your hand ...
    slowly and softly ... your word ... to freedom ...
And with it he presses the freeing energy ... the freeing power of his
    Holy Spirit into you ...
So that you may let go of what holds you back ...
So that you may forgive yourself for all the foolish doubts ... forgive yourself
    for all the hesitations and reluctances ...
So that you might accept this wonderful person God has created ...

And loved … by God … that you might love this creation called "you"
    the same way God does …
Be at peace …

Feel the freeing power of Christ's Spirit move through you …
Freeing you …
So that you feel weightless … buoyant … and able to float …
The power of Christ's Spirit …
Giving you new strength … and delight …
Delight …

Rest in the warm, loving arms of God …
You have been given a certain glow … that begins to shimmer …
    and illuminate you … and pushes out all the darkness …
Whatever held you back from your family or from those at school (or work)
    and even from yourself … has melted …
The Spirit of the Lord is your strength … and your light …
Jesus promises that in this new freedom … he will do wonderful things
    with you … together … always …
Be at peace with your newfound freedom …
At peace …

When you are ready …
Return to this time and place …
Come back to the group …
And know that you are not alone …
Come back with the light of your new freedom … and the Spirit of the Lord …
Who will free you to fulfill the Lord's great plan …
When you are ready you may open your eyes …
And be free …
Free.

Meditation Eight

The House Divided

Taking a journey with Jesus to the home we grew up in, we discover there, in spite of their flaws, great qualities in each of our family members. Then we find that the seed of each of their great qualities has also been planted in us. Inspired by Luke 11:17, 18a, 20-23. The use of relaxation technique two is suggested. Time: 14 minutes

And we pray:
Eternal God ...
Protector and Creator of families ...
Your gift of life is handed on to us through the blessing of children ...
It takes shape through the relationships in our families ...
We pray that you send us your Holy Spirit as we meditate today ...
That we might have new sight ... to see clearly ... those gifts with which
    you bless us in our own families ...
The gifts that can shape us ... and mold us with your love ...
Re-created with your love ...
Your love ...

With your eyes still closed ...
Take a journey ...
Perhaps a familiar journey ...
To a place that you sometimes escape to ...
A place where you go to get away from your family ...
Where nothing can bother you ...
Where you can find *yourself* ... and be at peace ...
Take a journey to that place once more ...
Where you can be alone ...
Where nothing can harm you ... and you feel very safe ...
Alone ... and at peace ...
Peace ...

Look around you ...
Take a deep breath ... and just relax ...
Is the scent familiar ... or is it something new? ...
Can you hear anything? ...
Is it familiar? ... or something new? ...
What do you see around you? ...

69

Over there ...
Someone is sitting ... with their back to you ...
Drawing on the ground ... with a stick ...
Wide sweeping lines ... a circle here ... an arc there ...
With his back to you ...
He probably knows you are approaching ...
 but he's being patient ... quiet ...
Waiting for you to join him ...
And as you come closer to him ... you find there's a kind of tranquility
 in the air ... a feeling of understanding and compassion ...
He seems to be radiating a kind of love ... love beyond
 human understanding ...
And as you stand behind him ... you can feel that warmth ...
 not on your hand or face ...
But an incredible warmth deep within ... within the soul ...
You reach out your hand to touch his shoulder ... and he presses the side of his
 face to it ...
He stands ... and turns ... and the smiling face of Jesus meets you ...
 eye to eye ... heart to heart ... soul to soul ...
And he wraps his arms around you ... and you can feel the power of
 his love ...
You know that he's been waiting ... patiently ... for you ...
Be at peace ...
Peace ...

As he steps back ... he smiles again ... and tells you about some of his
 happiest memories when he was growing up in his family ...
Some of the best memories of his family ...
And sometimes ... he remembers ... it wasn't easy ... but some of those
 memories were the best ...
Be still ... and try to hear him tell you of his happiest memory ...
 with his family ...
Just be still and listen very closely ...
Very closely ...

And the Lord asks you about yours ...
He asks you about your happiest memory growing up in your family ...
A special time you could never forget ...
A great time when you wished it would always be like that ...
 but somehow it never was ...
But for that brief time ... it was great ... you will never forget it ...
Quietly ... slowly ... share that with Jesus ...

70

And his eyes seem to widen with excitement …
He smiles in that special way that lets you know he understands …
As if he had been there all the time …
And understood …

Jesus takes you by the hand …
He asks you to take him to your home … the place where your family lived
    while you were growing … maturing …
That place of memories …
Hold the Lord's hand tightly and take him to the home where you grew up
    with your family …
You can walk if you want … or you can run … or even fly … or just
    blink your eyes … until you're standing in front of that old house …
You can point out to the Lord the things about the house that you
    remember most …
Perhaps you'll point out the window of your room … or the door that
    you always used … or the window that got broken or perhaps
    never worked right …

Take the Lord by the hand … and bring him into the house …
    maybe by walking right through the front door … or the back door …
    without even having to open it …
Bring the Lord into the house …
Show him around … in a kind of silence …
Because suddenly you realize … nobody seems to notice you …
They don't hear you … or see you …
It's as if you are there with Jesus and nobody knows …
    except you and the Lord …

Take the Lord … by the hand … to the room where you are most likely
    to find your mother … from long ago …
Can you tell what she is wearing? … what she is doing? …
Jesus asks about her …
About a time when there was tension … or a misunderstanding …
    and people got stubborn …
Maybe you said something you really didn't mean … but you were
    afraid to tell her that you didn't mean it …
And there were hurt feelings …
Jesus nods his head in understanding …
He knows … it is so difficult … it happens …
Then he asks you to think real hard …
About what you feel is her best gift … her best talent … the ability she had
    to do a certain something … something that at times you relied on …

71

What was the very best thing that she did for you? ...
Jesus goes to your mother ... gives her a big hug ...
And thanks her for that special talent ... the something that made your life
    a little better ...
How she was special to you ...
And Jesus gives her another big hug ...
Is there anything you would like to say to your mother? ...
Anything you would like to do? ...
Simply be at peace ...
At peace ...

Now take the Lord by the hand again ...
This time take him to the room where you would usually expect to
    find your father ...
And now you stand there ... you and Jesus and your father ...
And again ... the Lord asks you to tell him about one of the difficult times
    you might have had with your father ...
When nobody listened ... because both of you were too busy speaking ...
    or yelling ... and nothing could get resolved ... at least not
    resolved your way ...
And you felt kind of tense inside ... almost like it was too much and you
    could explode ... but you had to hold firm ... because he didn't try
    to understand ...
He couldn't understand ...

Jesus remembers a time in his youth when his parents didn't understand
    him ... when they found him in the temple ... and they didn't under-
    stand that he had lost track of the time ... they thought he was
    lost ... it wasn't intentional ... but they were still very upset ...
And he understands those difficult times ... and nods ...
He asks you what good thing you will always remember about your father ...
What special quality or ability does he have that helps you so much? ...
What can you depend on ... that you would like to have for yourself ...
What is the one special thing you will always be grateful for? ...
Again the Lord smiles that all-knowing smile ...
And goes to your father ... and thanks him for that ... and tells him
    how grateful he is ... and gives him a great big hug ...
Is there anything you would like to say to your father? ...
Anything you would like to do? ...
And be at peace ...
Peace ...

Then Jesus asks you to take him to the other person in the house ...
     a brother or a sister ... or the brother or sister that you always hoped for ...
And standing there now with you ... and the Lord ... is that sibling ...
Jesus asks you how you get into trouble together ...
He asks about those times when you lose patience with each other ...
And you drive each other to frustration ...
And you think that you must have been cursed to be stuck with each other ...
Jesus laughs ... out loud ... because he can hear so much love
     hidden in all those words ...
Love that just doesn't know how to get out ...
So you both struggle ...
He knows how much you are envied by the other ...
And looked up to ... and admired ...
He knows how difficult it is to admit all those things ...
And how much easier it is to blast each other away ...
He knows ... and he understands ...

Jesus asks what you really like best about that sibling ...
What is the one special quality that is really so great? ...
     what quality might you miss if it weren't there? ...
What is there in them that shows the greatest potential? ...
And again ... the Lord goes to that person ... cuddles his arms around them
     and thanks them for just being themselves ...
Created specially by his heavenly Father ... with so much love ...
Is there anything you would like to say to that sibling? ...
Anything you would like to do? ...
Be at peace ...
Peace ...

Now ... with the Lord's hand firmly in yours ... take him to a room in your
     home where you can find an important relative ...
One member of your larger family ... that has always been
     so very important to you ...
One relative that has gone out of their way for you ... or treated you
     very specially ...
Or that you just like more than anyone else ... one you are glad to
     be able to call a relative ...
As you stand there with Jesus and that favorite relative ... explain to the Lord
     what makes this person so special ... what quality do they have
     that you admire so much? ...

The Lord smiles ... nods his head a few times ... and you know how lucky you
    are to have this great person in your life ...
Then Jesus goes to that person ... thanks them for being so patient with you ...
    for understanding you so much ... for caring about you with
    such admiration ...
And the Lord gives that relative a great big hug ... a great big hug ...
Is there anything you would like to say to this special relative? ...
Is there anything you would like to do?
And be at peace ...
At peace ...

Then Jesus turns to you ...
He tells you to look deep in yourself ...
And if you look hard enough ... you can find all those qualities of each of
    your family members ... right there inside of you ...
Look deep inside ... and you'll find that same quality that makes your
    mother so great ... and the quality and ability of your father as well ...
    deep within ...
And keep looking and you will find that quality in you that makes you admire
    your brother or sister so much ...
And of course ... the gift from your favorite relative is in you as well ...
And all these qualities ... some you know of already ... and some you need to
    develop more strongly ...
These are the qualities God has given to you to help build your family,
    even stronger than it is now ...
Gifts and qualities of love ... that can make your family more than
    it's ever been ...
And you have the power and the gifts to make it happen ...
To bring love into your family in a new way ...
Is there anything you would like to say to the Lord? ...
Is there anything you would like to do? ...
Be at peace ...

When you are ready ...
Leave the memories of your home ...
But bring with you those special gifts ...
And return here bringing those qualities with you ...
When you are ready you may open your eyes ...
But please don't try to make contact with anyone ...
Just spend a few minutes reflecting on those great qualities that are
    still with you ... ready to be used to help others ...
And be at peace ...
Peace.

Meditation Nine

The Lord's Prayer

With Jesus as our guide, we explore our personal ideas about God and reflect on the meaning of the Lord's Prayer in our life. Inspired by Matthew 6:6-15. The use of relaxation technique two is suggested. Time: 14 minutes

And we pray:
Almighty and Merciful God …
In our loneliness you have called to us …
Pleaded with us to be in communion with you …
And we want to respond …
To fulfill your invitation …
To know you … to be with you … in prayer …
Please … send us your living Spirit …
That we may be joined with you …
That we may learn from you …
To pray as we have never prayed before …
To begin again …
Again …

With your eyes still closed …
Let the Spirit of God lead you …
To a place of solitude …
Where you can be all alone …
A place of peace …
A place where you might be able to find … and recognize God …
A place where you can invite God to be …
A place where you can be still … with God's Spirit …
A place where you can be safe … and still … and alone …
     and nothing can harm you …
Where you can be quietly aware of the Spirit's movement …
Aware of the silent breath of God's Spirit …
Breathing life …
Breathing in tune with your life …
Quietly … in and out …
Be still … just slowly breathing with God's Spirit …
In and out … peacefully …
Slowly breathing in rhythm with God …
Slowly …

And be at peace …
Peace …

Realize that you are not alone …
For not far from you …
Is Jesus …
Sitting with his head lowered …
Jesus … with eyes closed from distractions … hands folded in gratitude …
Praying …
He hears you … he must have been waiting for you …
And he looks up … smiles …
And reaches a hand toward you …
Inviting you …
Welcoming you to come and sit with him …

Jesus moves over … to make room for you … to join him …
And gives you a big welcoming hug …
You can feel the close protection of God …
Jesus … who would never let anything harm you …
Who is keeping you safe …
And be at peace in the protective arms of the Lord …
At peace …

Jesus whispers …
To tell you a secret …
He tells you that at the heart of his strength is prayer …
His source of confidence and decision making is prayer …
As long as he remains close to his Father in heaven through prayer …
He is filled with power … with great joy …
Filled with the happiness and confidence that comes only from
    union with God …
And Jesus wants to share this … to teach you to pray …
Is there anything you want to say to the Lord? …
Anything you would like to do? …

Jesus slowly and gently cups his hands over your head …
Strong hands … but very gentle …
Hands with the purity of God …
And you can feel peace come over you …
Like a refreshing breeze …
His peace flows over you …
He slowly slides his hands down over your face …
Closing your eyes with his fingers …

76

Gently …
And he asks you to be still …
With your eyes closed …

He asks you to find the place inside you that can hear silent music …
The place you might call your heart … or maybe your soul …
But that special place where the hearts of others are understood …
The place that has known the silent thrill of joy … or love … or the
      bitter tears of rejection and hurt … or loneliness …
The place deep within you that feels life …
Suddenly … as if the Lord himself touched this special place within you …
      there is a feeling of holiness …
A special place that is sacred …
A place to meet and talk with God …

Jesus says that it will be here that you will hear the voice of God …
Here that you can pour out your prayer …
And also receive a prayer from God …
Here … in a special place that is sacred.

Jesus begins … talking silently in this sacred place …
Within you …
And asks … to *you* … Who is God? … for *you* … Who is God? …
      What is God like? …
Jesus explains that for *him* … God is like a father … a loving, caring father …
But for *you* … What is God like for you? …
Jesus asks you to tell God exactly that …
This is the beginning of your prayer … to express your image of God …
And be at peace …

Then Jesus asks you … where do *you* find God? …
Jesus shares with you that *he* finds God wherever it has been made sacred …
      pure … wherever there is love … wherever he can be in communion
      with God …
For Jesus … that is heaven …
But where do *you* find God? …
And now … in your prayer … talk about all the different places where you
      find God … speak to God from within your heart …
Think where you best find God … and then thank God for being there
      for you …
And be at peace …

Jesus whispers to you again … What is God like for *you?* …
For him, Jesus tells you that God is sacred … holy … hallowed …
Even God's name is sacred … holy … hallowed …
But … for *you* … What is God like? …
How would you describe the God that you know? …
And then speak to God in your heart … tell what God is like for you …
Quietly … gently … tell God …
And be at peace …
Peace …

Jesus turns to you …
He speaks softly … telling you that his primary work is to bring God's reign
    into this world …
And that he even prays for it to come …
Jesus prays … that he will be helped in bringing about the reign of God …
He needs the strength only God can give …
But what is the work God has invited *you* to do? …
What is it that you believe should happen? …
What would you like God's help in doing? …
And Jesus asks you to pray the words in the silence of your soul …
    that sacred place deep within you …
Like a song that only God can hear …
Let the words pour out of you and into the heart of God …
With your desire for God … your desire to do God's work … in this world …
And be at peace …
Peace …

Jesus smiles with a sort of teasing confidence and then gazes away …
    as if dreaming the possible …
And he tells you that he has made it possible for heaven to be united
    with earth … here …
He has made it possible for this earth to be like heaven …
But he can't do it alone …
Jesus tells you that in heaven …
God's will has already been established …
And if this world would surrender to the will of God … well …
    then it would be heaven here! …
Heaven and earth united …
Jesus tells you is what he prays for … that is his dream … that
    this earth will be transformed … that heaven would come to this world …
That earth would be like heaven …
And Jesus asks you … What is *your* dream? … the dream that is possible
    with God? …

Quietly ... in your heart ... share that dream with God ...
And be at peace ...

Jesus tells you that when he prays ... he asks to have his basic needs
　　taken care of ... his daily bread ... his essentials for life ...
So he can be free from that worry ... free to give his attention to others ...
And he asks you ... What is *your* basic need? ... What is essential for *you*
　　that causes *you* to worry? ...
What can you ask God to take care of for you ... so you will be free
　　from worry? ...
What is your basic need? ...
And now ... ask God to provide ...
Quietly ... gently ...
At peace ...

Jesus turns to you again and begins to talk ...
Jesus tells you that most people worry ... worry about their guilt ...
　　worry about their mistakes ... and this worry holds them back ...
We worry about how people have hurt us ... or how we have hurt
　　someone else ...
Jesus reminds you that God's greatest gift is forgiveness ...
　　which destroys worry ...
And Jesus asks ... Who has hurt *you?* ... Who is in need of *your*
　　forgiveness? ...
And in the quiet of your heart ... Jesus asks you to see that person
　　who has hurt you ... or the person you may have hurt ...
Jesus asks you to see the person that may be the source of your guilt or hurt ...
The person that might also be hurting ... but would never let you know ...
The person that shares the guilt ... the hurt ... the pain ...
And also needs your understanding ... your help ... your forgiveness ...

God can give you the strength to break free ...
Because God too wants to forgive ...
And will forgive ... but in the same way that we forgive others ...
It is as if you must show God *how* you want to be forgiven ...
To make the forgiveness complete ...
For there is power in forgiveness ...
Your forgiveness for God's forgiveness ...
Look at that person who is hurting as well ... who needs your help ...
Is there anything you want to say to them? ...
Anything you want to do? ...

Is there anything you want to say to the Lord? …
Anything you want to do? …
And be at peace …

With the power of forgiveness comes the power of God's protection …
    protection from whatever might come between us and God …
Jesus asks what has distracted you from God's love and God's power? …
What has kept God at a distance from you when you have really needed him
    most and not even known it? …
Quietly in your heart … ask God for the protection to deliver you from the
    need of whatever distracts you from experiencing God's love …
And quietly rest with God …
Be at peace … like God's own child … curl up and rest in the arms of God …
    who loves you and protects you … and gives you the power …
    for forgiveness …
Is there anything else you want to say to God? …
Anything else you want to do? …
And be at peace …

Listen in the quiet of the sacred place within you …
Listen to hear what God would want you to feel …
    would want you to know …
And be at peace with God …
Feel the Lord holding you … protecting you …
And know that the Lord will always be there …
And be at peace with God …

When you are ready …
Come back … with the confidence of God's union …
    with the presence of God …
And God's peace …
And know you are not alone …
There are others here who share that same need to pray …
    to be quietly in union with God … and with you …
When you are ready you may open your eyes …
And know that you are not alone …
And be at peace …
Peace.

Meditation Ten

The Treasures That Last

We remember the special people in our lives who have taught us about hope, faith, and love—the treasures that last and bring us closer to God. Inspired by Matthew 6:19-21. The use of relaxation technique one is suggested.
Time: 14 minutes

And we pray:
O eternal and ever-living God …
Who has no beginning or end …
We open ourselves to you in this time of prayer …
May we enter into your wisdom …
Guided by your Holy Spirit …
May we discover those things in our passing life that have drawn us to you …
And those things that have kept us apart …
With the eternal hope …
That we might one day step from this passing world …
Into your kingdom that is everlasting …
To also become everlasting …
With you …

And with your eyes still closed …
Take a journey back …
A journey through your memories …
Of yesterday and the yesterdays before that …
Journey back through your memories to a time when you felt very content …
A time when you were pleased … at ease …
Maybe a few days ago … several years ago … maybe when you were
    much younger …
A time when you were satisfied with the life God had given you …

Journey back through your memories to that place where you felt peaceful …
With no worries …
Where no harm could come to you … and you knew you were very safe …
Feel the peace from that memory once more … that contentment …
    that sense of satisfaction …
When was that time? … and where? …
Find yourself there once again …
And look around you …

What are the different things near you? …
Beside you? …
Behind you? …
Is it warm? … or cool? …
Is it light? … or is it dark? …
And be at peace … alone … and very content with your memory …
Satisfied …

With this memory of contentment …
Kneel down … sit back on your heels … and close your folded hands
    onto your lap …
With your eyes closed … in the silence of your heart …
Whisper the name of the Lord …
Whisper an invitation for Jesus to come to you …
To be present with you …

Feel the gentle palm of the Lord's hand brush against the back of your head …
To rest at the nap of your neck … to rest on your shoulder …
Feel the warmth of the Lord's presence …
Loving … gentle … reassuring …
The Lord stands next to you …
The Lord who delights in being with you …
Who feels blessed … when invited to be with you …

Jesus quietly joins you … kneeling with you … facing you …
He wraps *his* hands around *your* praying hands …
And says that these four hands in prayer are like you and him … together …
    as you should be …
But you aren't always …

Jesus looks at you gently …
With an all-knowing contentment …
And says that you and he could do so much together …
Together …
He could help you … even more … if you would only let him …
He wants to help you more … even with the smallest things …
Then … holding your hands in his …
He tells you that he needs you … needs you to help him more …
To bring God's love … his love … into this world …
Making this world more like heaven … sacred … holy …
Together you and he could make the kingdom of God real … now …
    right here …

Just imagine … the kingdom of God …
There is so much that you and he could do together …
Together …

But things get in the way …
Things separate the two of you …
Distractions come between you …
Other priorities get in the way …
The Lord says that he doesn't want to intrude on those things …
He doesn't want to interfere … to be a bother to you …
Jesus tells you that he still wants to be there … for you …
    but only as often as you want …
As often as you let him …
As often as you invite him …
Is there anything you want to say to the Lord? …
Anything you would like to do? …

Jesus asks you to help him find those things that have gotten in the way …
The things you worried about …
The things that were so important … but broke …
The important thing that needed to be repaired … that was never right even
    after it was fixed …
It just didn't seem the same … or so important either …

Search through your memories to find that favorite thing you were
    so proud of …
That wore out … that got old … maybe out of style …
    and you have almost forgotten about …
But it was so very important … so long ago … you needed it so badly …
    and now … it's almost forgotten …
Discarded … thrown out … gone …
Gone …

When you were younger … maybe you had a special toy … that was so very
    important … that was worth the whole world … that you had stayed awake
    thinking about … hoping about …
That too is gone … worn … finished …

Think about something that you don't use anymore … it just sits there
    alone … rejected … finished … rejected …
The excitement is faded … your enthusiasm gone …
And that's alright … important things change … sometimes distracting us …
    keeping us preoccupied …

Perhaps there is someone else that could get new joy from it ... rather than it
    just sitting there ... alone ... rejected ...

Of all the things that were so important ... what has happened to them? ...
Those things that were distractions from God ... that briefly separated you
    from God ... briefly got in the way ...
Then Jesus tells you that there are other things that never fade ...
    or deteriorate ...
Great things that can bring you closer to him ...
Treasures that will last forever ... even an eternity ...
And the Lord presses his forehead against yours ...
    as if you might remember together ...
The Lord asks you to search through your memories for these
    special treasures ...
The Lord asks you to remember ...

Remember a special person in your life that offered you a special kindness ...
    when they did something for you that you never expected ...
And now they stand there ... with you and the Lord ...
And Jesus thanks them for that special kindness ...
Is there anything you want to say to them? ...
Anything you would like to do? ...

Jesus asks you to search your memories for a person that forgave you ...
    when they really didn't have to ...
A time in your life when someone was willing to forgive and forget ...
And not hold grudges against you ...
Now that person is standing here ... with you and the Lord ...
Jesus thanks them for sharing his mercy and gives that person a
    great big hug ...
For showing you such loving forgiveness ...
Is there anything you want to say to that person? ...
Anything you want to do? ...

Jesus asks you to search through your memories again ...
This time to find a certain hope that seemed to keep you going ...
    even when you wanted to give up ...
Think of a special time when you were frustrated and tired and felt like
    you had been pushed to your limit ...
When everything seemed foolish ...
When you thought your dream would never happen ...
But somehow you had hope ... it seemed like a silly kind of perseverance ...
    determination ... maybe even stubbornness ...

You wouldn't give up for the world ... you wouldn't ...
    because of some strange encouragement ...
And it paid off ...

Who gave you that sense of hope? ... taught you to never give up ...
    to hold on to that hope ...
Who was the person that touched your life with hope ... taught it to you? ...
Now they stand there ... with you and the Lord ...
Jesus thanks them for making the Father's hope so real ...
    and gives that person a great big hug ...
Is there anything you would like to say to that person? ...
Anything you would like to do? ...

Jesus asks you to search through your memories again ...
This time you must search for someone you trusted in ...
Someone you had confidence in ...
Confidence that they would come through for you ...
Perhaps when others doubted them ... you relied on them ... you had faith ...
And it paid off ... your confidence was not in vain ...
Standing there now is the person you had confidence in ...
    with you and the Lord ...
Jesus thanks this person for helping you discover the gift of faith ...
And the Lord gives them a great big hug ...
Is there anything you would like to say to that person? ...
Anything you would like to do? ...

Jesus asks you to search through your memories one last time ...
This time to search for a special moment ... a special time ...
    when you did a great deed for someone else ...
And no one ever found out that you were the person who should have
    gotten the credit ...
You did it ... not to get glory for yourself ... but because you knew it was
    the right thing to do for someone else ...
You could feel good about it ... all by yourself ...
Without a lot of praise ... without a lot of credit ...
Jesus holds you in his arms and tells you that he knows ...
He has always known ... and he knows how special you are ...
How capable you are ... how many times you have done things for him ...
Times that he is with you ...
Working with you ...
Together ...

And he is very proud of you …
This is the image and likeness of goodness that you were made in …
    in his goodness …

In his hope … in his faith … and in his love …
These are the treasures that last …
These are the treasures with which you have gifted others …
    because God has gifted you …
These are the treasures that are the building blocks of the kingdom of God …
The treasures that make heaven real … here … now … this very day …
Because of you …
Allowing God to work with you … in you … and through you …
The Lord is so very proud of you …
And holds you close …

Jesus promises to continue to be with you … and work through you …
If you work for what lasts …
If you work for what doesn't wear out … or break …
    or get lost on a shelf or tucked away …
For you know what the important things in this world truly are …
    those things for God and from God …
Yours …
With the Lord …
Together …
Like your hands together … with his in prayer …
Together in prayer …
And be at peace …

When you are ready …
Leave those memories … those treasures that will never fade …
And come back here …
Knowing you are not alone …
There are others around you who are committed to bringing
    the kingdom of God into this world … with you …
When you are ready …
Come back here …
And open your eyes …
But I would ask that you don't look at anyone or talk to anyone …
Just reflect for a moment on all that you experienced …
All that you thought about …
All of the people that you met in those memories …
And be at peace …
Peace.

On Anxiety

Letting go of worry, we trust in God. Inspired by Matthew 6:25-34. The use of relaxation technique four is suggested. Time: 14 minutes

And we pray:
Almighty Father in heaven …
Our world gets more and more complicated …
The demands on us become greater …
We are pushed to race faster and faster …
And in desperation we try to gain control …
Only to lose ourselves … losing sight of you …
Being crushed with anxiety and worry …
Send us your Holy Spirit as we pray …
That we might become free …
Free to let go of the worry …
And gain strength from our trust in you …
To trust in you …

And with your eyes still closed …
Take a journey …
Far … far … away …
A journey to a special garden …
A garden you have never seen before …
Where you can be alone …
And very safe …
Where no harm can come to you …
And nothing can hurt you …
A special garden where you can be alone and at peace …
At peace …

A garden where all the plants are lush and healthy …
Where the flowers are strong and beautiful …
Where it is peaceful …
Your own garden … where you can feel at home … and at peace …
And be still …
With your eyes still closed … take a deep breath …
And taste the sweet air …
The air filled with the light perfume of flowers …

Cool and clean ...
Almost intoxicating ...
Your garden ... a place where you can belong ... and feel safe ...
Over there ... around that bush ... you can hear someone working in the soil ...
Someone who is gently tilling the soil with his hands ...
Joyfully planting a small flower ... carefully supporting it until it
    grows strong on its own ...
And you slowly walk toward the gardener ...
You can only see his back ... bent over on his knees ... working in the earth ...
As you walk closer ... you can feel a kind of peace coming from him ...
    a gentle caring ...
He spends his whole life keeping this magnificent garden in order ...
    healthy ... strong ... for you ...

Now you stand behind him ... quietly ... watching ...
He stops ... he doesn't turn around to you ...
But he knows that you are there ...
He opens his arms ... as if sweeping the entire view of the garden ...
And he tells you that all this is for you ...
That he wants to do all this for you ...
Then slowly he turns around ... and looks up at you ...
And you can see the smiling face of Jesus ...
He asks if you like what he has done ...
What he has done for you ...
For you ...
Is there anything you would like to say to him? ...
Anything you would like to do? ...

Jesus stands up and gently wraps his arms around you ...
He hugs you because he knows you are so special ...
More precious than any of the magnificent flowers of the garden ...
Listen to what the Lord has to tell you ...
Be at peace ... and listen ...
With the Lord ... at peace ...

Jesus wraps his hand around yours ... he wants to give you a
    tour of the garden ...
He begins walking with you ... leading you back to the earlier part
    of the garden ...
Around the bushes ... past the trees ...
To another time ... to another place ...
Some time in the past with your family ...
When you were filled with worry ...

And you were afraid things wouldn't work out ...
When you were upset and didn't know what to do ...
And ... as if walking through a door ... you are now standing there again ...
    in that same scene ... with your family ...
Except now you can watch it from a distance ... standing next to Jesus ...
    his hand with yours ...
And the fear is gone ... but you can remember the anxiety and worry ...
    when you were afraid things wouldn't work out ...
Now ... turn to the Lord ... and tell him what is happening ...
Explain to the Lord ... who cares so much for you ...
    the feelings that are inside you during this time of worry ...

The Lord understands ... he knows what you are going through ...
He holds you close ... to protect you ... so you won't be harmed ...
You feel the safety of his love ...
Be at peace ...

Then Jesus shows you how it turned out ...
He shows you what he did ... even if it didn't make sense ...
He shows you how he later brought some good out of a difficult situation ...
Quietly ... so intimately ... he explains what he did to take care of you ...
How he was watching out for you ... caring for you ...
And be at peace ...
Peace ...
Is there anything you want to say to Jesus? ...
Is there anything you would like to do? ...

Know how precious you are to him ... how important you are to God ...
The Lord again takes you by the hand ... and leads you to another
    area of the garden ... where he has worked ... and nurtured the
    young growth ... to grow strong and healthy ...
Your growth ...
In your garden ...
Jesus takes you to another area ... to another time ... to another situation ...
When you were at school (or at work) ...
When you were perhaps impatient ... or you were apprehensive or uneasy ...
A time when you were very concerned ... and faced with a
    very difficult situation ...
When you thought you knew how things could turn out ...
    how things were supposed to turn out ...
You are there again ... going through another door ... watching as a
    bystander ... looking at the situation again ...

But this time with the security of Jesus … the Lord who remains
    faithful to you …
Explain the situation to Jesus … tell him how you feel about this occasion …
    the situation that was causing you turmoil inside … your anxiety …
Tell him what was going on inside of you during this whole thing …
Help him to feel the feelings that were inside of you …
The feelings running around inside of you …

Jesus holds your hand firmly …
And assures you that he understands … he knows …
He's felt the same kind of feelings as well …
Then he points to the scene … and shows you what he was doing
    during that time …
He explains how he was looking after you …
Then Jesus shows you the good that came out of that for you …
He tells you how that situation has brought you to this day … to this time
    in your life … to unfold the good things of your life …
    to help you open to him …
How he has been watching out for you all the time …
    even when you didn't realize it …
He draws you close … and reassures you of his deepest devotion to you …
    and of God's love that protects you …
Be at peace … in the arms of Jesus …
At peace …

Jesus wants to continue his tour through your garden …
With your hands together … with the security of God's dedication to you …
Jesus continues walking through the garden …
    slowly walking around bushes … passing flowers …
Circling back … closer to where you found him working in the earth …
    when he was bent over planting new flowers …
Jesus brings you back to a more recent time …
To an event that has happened in the recent past …
To a time when you recently felt plagued by a situation that
    wasn't going right …
To an event where you were troubled and perplexed …
Maybe fearful or perhaps angry …
When you felt like nothing was going to work out the way it was
    supposed to …
Maybe you felt like you had lost control of the situation …
Maybe there was nothing you could do … you were helpless …
You were caught up in so much worry …

But the anxiety didn't help …

Again … you stand with the Lord … outside the situation … looking on … remembering all the frustration …

Remembering the confusion …

And the Lord asks you … in a quiet voice … to tell him what is happening … from your perspective … the way you see it … the way that you are feeling it …

Is there anything you want to say to the Lord? …

Is there anything you would like to do? …

Know that Jesus is with you in a very special way … listening … hearing … feeling it with you …

Jesus tells you how he was with you all that time … taking care of you …

He would never let it destroy you …

Jesus asks you what you gained from that time …

What did you learn? …

With the Lord to help you …

To be with you …

How have you become better … because of it? …

Jesus walks with you … through the garden … hand in hand … together in the cool of the evening …

Back to where he was planting the seedlings … when you first met him …

He tells you that he was getting this new area ready … putting it in order already …

That this is a time of worry and anxiety that is yet to come …

A new situation where you might become filled with anxiety again …

There isn't even a door yet … that you can enter … and see …

Yet the Lord is caring for you even before you need his help …

He is already there … preparing goodness … making things better for you … better than even you could make for yourself …

Jesus tells you that the worrying has never been beneficial … or productive …

That all your worrying throughout your life has gotten you nothing …

If you can let go of the worry … Jesus can replace it … with trust …

Trust in him … trust that he has been taking good care of you … in the past …

Trust in his promise that he could never let go of you …

That you are too valuable to him … too special for him to let anything happen to you …

Trust that he will continue to care for you …

And be at peace …

Is there anything you would like to say to the Lord? …
Is there anything you would like to do? …

Rest in God's love … rest in the Lord's devotion to you and his caring
    for you …
With peace and confidence …
Jesus holds out to you his gift of trust …
He asks for an exchange … an exchange of your worry for his trust …
Be at peace … holding the gift of trust close to you …
To be with you forever …

When you are ready … bring the gift of trust back with you …
Leave the garden … and return here … bringing that gift of trust with you …
Know that you're not alone …
There are others here … around you … that can share their gift of trust …
Knowing that Jesus will take care of you no matter what the situation …
Be at peace …
Knowing that with this new gift of trust in the Lord …
    you will be able to get through anything …
For there is nothing to worry about …
Nothing to worry you …
Be at peace …

When you are ready you may open your eyes …
But continue to remain quiet …
Just reflect for a few moments on all the Lord has shown you
    in your prayer …
All the Lord has told you in your prayer …
And be at peace …
Peace.

Meditation Twelve

Judge Not

We discover the cyclical pain of judging and imposing expectations on others, while learning from God how his gift of acceptance can break that chain. Inspired by Matthew 7:1-5. The use of relaxation technique two is suggested. Time: 10 minutes

And we pray:
Almighty God …
Who watches over us with compassion and forgiveness …
You ask us to love one another …
To care for one another …
But your plea to us is often too difficult …
Sometimes we meet each other with fear and apprehension …
Afraid of ridicule … afraid of rejection by others …
So we become protective … defensive …
We meet each other with armor … fortified with caution and mistrust …
Hiding the love … Hiding the care …
Almighty God … help us to break through …
Guide us as we pray with your Spirit …
That we may learn from you …
That we may learn … to love one another openly …
As you love us …

With your eyes still closed …
Go to a place that is safe …
A place that is tranquil …
Where you can be all alone …
With nothing to harm you …
Or anything to distract you …
A place where you can be peaceful … and think things through …
And be at peace …
Peace …

Look around you … become familiar with everything …
With the safety of the place …
And with the solitude …
A chance to be alone with yourself …
And be at peace …

The more you realize the solitude ... the being alone ...
The more you realize that the Lord is with you ...
He is part of the solitude ...
Away from all the distractions ...
With you ... together ... alone ...
And be at peace ....
Is there anything you want to say to Jesus? ...
Anything you would like to do? ...

Just the two of you in your solitude ... in the quiet ...
In the peace ... the serenity ...
Jesus asks if you trust him completely ...
For he would never let anything harmful happen to you when
    the two of you are alone ...
Can you trust him completely? ...
For Jesus has a very special gift ...
If you are patient ...
If you can trust ...
Jesus holds you close ... protectively in himself ...
Close to the compassion of his heart ... the compassion that seems to
    soak through to you ... from the Lord ...
And be at peace ...

Jesus asks you to think back through your memories to a time ...
A time when you were hurt by an older relative ...
Maybe in an argument with an aunt or an uncle ...
Maybe when there was hurt or anger with one of your parents ...
When you felt they were critical ...
Or they were hurtful ...
When they were cruel or sharp with you ...
Unintentionally ...
Perhaps not even realizing it ...
When they judged you wrongly ...

Take Jesus by the hand to that place ... that place where there was pain ...
Show Jesus the different things around you ...
Now point out to the Lord ... the person who hurt you ...
Listen to that person as they get upset ... or compare you to
    something else ... or to someone else ...
Hear the accusations ...
What are they trying to say? ...
What is it that you hear ... even if they don't intend it? ...

What is your response? …
Is there anything you say to them? …
Is there anything you do? …

Jesus stands there with you … and listens …
Sadly … his head bowed low … he listens … quietly … still …
You can turn to the Lord …
See the expression on his face …
And you can feel his silence …

The Lord turns to you … his eyes look questioning …
He wants to understand …
He wants to know …
He wants to hear from you … what is inside … what is happening to you …
Softly … slowly … take a deep breath …
Hold it a few seconds …
Silently let the breath leave …
Another silent breath …
And slowly … softly … tell the Lord …
Tell Jesus the thoughts you had … the feelings that scrambled around
    inside of you …
Trust the Lord who is carefully listening …
Who understands …
Explain the hurt … the rejection … the bitterness …
Maybe even the confusion … of being unsure …

And Jesus understands …
He understands …
He holds you … and comforts you …
Silently he comforts you …
Not saying anything yet …
He just holds you … gently rocking you in his arms …
And you know that it will be alright …
Gently rocking in the arms of the Lord …
Is there anything more you would like to say to the Lord? …
Is there anything more you would like to do? …
And be at peace …
Peace …

Then Jesus draws back … to look at you … reassures you with a small smile …
The Lord wants to take you someplace special …
Back in time …
A generation earlier …

To when the adult that had hurt you … was young like you …
Jesus takes you by the hand to a time when that adult was with their parent …
You can watch from a distance …
A time of an argument like yours …
A time of anger and hurt …
You stand there watching the adult that had hurt you …
    that had said things to you …
Standing there with their parents … hearing almost the same thing
    when they were your age …
And you know that they were learning … from them …
You can almost see inside them … feelings they can't hide from you …
Feelings of being criticized … judged by unfair expectations … ridiculed …
You can sense their feelings of being betrayed …
    the anger they used to try to stop their hurt …
Feelings of confusion …
Their feelings are similar to yours …

You can hear their parent's words … the accusations …
The sharp words of judgment … criticism …
They are overly critical … faultfinding …
All that relative wants is to be understood … but nobody has learned …
No one has taught them to be patient … to understand …
Then there is silence …

And Jesus slowly nudges you toward this relative … this victim …
    this person that is being judged and humiliated by their parents …
    a person you now know as an adult …
But now they are your age … and they have been hurt and judged …
Jesus nudges you toward them …
Is there anything you can say to them? …
Is there anything you can do? …

Can you share your feelings with them? …
Help them to understand? …
Jesus holds both of you together …
Because he is so proud of you …
You and the person who will treat you poorly as they were treated one day …
Because they have never learned …

And Jesus asks you to go with him …
Go with him to another time …
Closer to now …

Maybe last month ...
Maybe yesterday ...
When you lost your patience with someone else ... someone that was
    irritating you ... a bother to you ...
Jesus takes you to a time when you confronted someone ...
    someone that got you upset ...
Maybe someone in your family ... or at school ... or at work ...
    or in your neighborhood ...
When you lost your patience ... and said things ... said painful words ...
And ridiculed ...
And judged ... and hurt them ...

And Jesus asks who they will hurt in turn ...
Who will they judge in turn? ...
Can the cycle be broken? ...
Who will learn to be patient? ... who will patiently accept? ...
Who will learn to compromise? ...
Who can take the first step to break the chain of punishing? ...

The Lord shows you the person who has listened to you ...
    most recently ...
As they stand there in silence ...
Stand there in their hurt ...
After you said those things ...
Again you can see inside of them ...
You can see their needs ... what they really wanted ...
And Jesus asks you if there is anything you can say to them? ...
In his name ... is there any way you can help them to
    learn all you have just learned? ...
To share the gift of God that you have been given? ...
Invite the Lord to join you ...
To be with you and the person who is hurting ...
Is there anything you want to share with Jesus? ...
Anything that he should know? ...

Jesus holds you closely ...
He is so very proud of you ...
You know that you have an incredible gift from God ...
A gift of patient compassion ...
A special part of God that you can carry with you ... forever ...
That you can use ... forever ...
And be at peace ...

With the Lord …
And the mutual gift you share …
Together …
And be at peace …

And when you are ready …
Leave that place of comfort …
That place of safety …
And come back here …
Bring that special gift of the Lord back with you …
And know that you are not alone …
You are with others who need that gift that God has given to you …
Others that need that patient compassion …
To heal them … while you are healed by sharing it …
And be at peace …

When you are ready you may open your eyes …
But don't look at anyone … or talk to anyone …
Just peacefully think about all that you have experienced …
All that you have been given …
And be at peace …
Peace.

Meditation Thirteen

"Who do you say that I am?"

We uncover our identity, which is found with Christ, the image and the likeness of God, whom we reflect. Inspired by Matthew 16:13-18. The use of relaxation technique three is suggested. Time: 14 minutes

And we pray:
All-knowing God …
Who has created all things and proclaimed them good …
Who has created us … and knows us completely …
We come before you placing ourselves in the hands of your Spirit …
That we might discover during our meditation …
Who we are to you …
That we might look at ourselves through your eyes …
And recognize your creative love …
That we might look at those around us … and find your creative love
      in them …

With your eyes still closed …
Take a journey to a very distant land … far away … to ancient Israel …
Journey to the outskirts of a small town …
Nestled between mountains …
On a dry dirt road … snaking around a cliff …
Parched and chapped by a blistering sun …
Ahead of you … a caravan of heavily burdened camels …
      wobbling on spindly legs is starting off on a long trek …

A road leads over and through jagged mountains …
Dotted and marked by isolated merchants … travelers on donkeys …
      people on foot …
All slowly moving along the road …
You can taste the dry dust …
Occasionally it is blown into twirling little clouds by a faint breeze …
You feel the sun's heat … burning through your clothes …
Hot … prickly … dry …
To your left … around a jagged rock … you see a clump of trees …
Low trees … wide and flat … but offering cool shade to a group of people …
      men and women … who sit beneath them … sharing a meal …

Not far away ... separate from the rest ... two men sit beneath a tree ...
    eating ... talking ...
You draw close to them ... quietly ... standing near ... just to listen ...
They're talking about the scriptures ... interpreting the different parts ...
The two men are intense ... thoughtful ... reflective ...
The younger man calls the other Jesus ... who smiles ...
    and nods his approval at something the younger man has said ...
You hear Jesus refer to the younger man as Peter ...
They are having a serious conversation ...
Quietly ... thoughtfully ... reflectively ...
Slowly everyone and everything dissolves ... disappears ...
    except the three of you ... sitting in the shade ...
And it is very still ... quiet ... just Jesus ... and Peter ... and you ...
You can hear them clearly ... and you listen quietly ...

Peter reminds Jesus of the time they fed the five thousand people ...
    sitting on a grassy hill ... in small groups ...
When the people were far from home ... hungry ...
Jesus was offered fish and bread by a young child ...
Jesus lifted them up to heaven ... blessed them ... distributed them ...
And suddenly there was more food than anyone needed ...
    more than enough for everyone ...

And Peter reminisces with the Lord about the woman who had
    many ... many sins ...
Who came to Jesus' table with great regret ...
Who knelt at his feet ... weeping ... crying ...
And with her tears ... with her love ... she washed the feet of Jesus ...
Wiping them dry with her hair ... lovingly ... with devotion ...
And her many sins were forgiven ... she was made pure ... loved by God ...
Loved by God ...

Peter tells Jesus ... he knows ... Jesus is the Messiah ...
He knows Jesus is the Lord ...

Then Jesus reaches to Peter ... anoints his forehead with his thumb ...
    and smiles ... and nods his approval ...
Peter shakes his head no ... and reminds Jesus of his many doubts in
    the past... of the time he doubted the Lord during the storm in the boat ...
    and that he is not worthy ... that now he does not deserve this kindness ...
Then again ... Peter reminds Jesus of his silly behavior when he jumped from
    the boat and tried to be like God walking on the water ... foolish and silly ...

And again … Peter reminds the Lord of when he had argued with the other
    disciples over who was the greatest … who would be the best in the
    kingdom of God … and he created jealousy and envy among them …
Peter shakes his head again no … he does not deserve to be anointed …
    he is not that holy … not that deserving …
But Jesus only smiles …
And with his hand … points to Peter's chest …
And tells him that there is great love there … there is great faith there …
Jesus smiles …
And with his hand … points to Peter's head …
There is great strength there … great determination …
You hear Jesus saying "You are solid … a leader … like a rock …
I shall call you Peter which means rock …
For my church shall be built with you as its foundation …
Strong … determined … with great faith and great love … like you …
With great love."

Then Jesus slowly turns to you …
Nods his head in approval … gently … with a wisdom that can see
    through you … deeply into you …
He nods his head in approval …
And takes your hand …
Raises it to his face … holds it against himself …
And asks you …
Who am I? … Who am I to you? …
With all that we have been through … together … he asks …
Who am I to you? …
Is there anything you would like to tell the Lord? …
Is there anything you would like to do? …

Jesus invites you to go back with him … to a time in your life when you
    did something for someone else …
No one knew about it … just you … you did a favor for someone else …
Maybe you never got any recognition from others …
But you did it because it was something you wanted to do …
Perhaps when someone was in need … and couldn't do everything
    for themselves …
Or when someone couldn't depend on others … and you decided to take care
    of things yourself … to help … to show you cared …
    to show your love …
You stand there watching the scene again …
And the Lord silently smiles … nods his head in approval …
Turns to you … anoints your forehead with his thumb … and smiles …

He holds you close with a hug …
Is there anything you would like to say to the Lord? …
Is there anything you would like to do? …

Jesus again invites you to another time when you had to forgive someone …
A time when you were filled with anger … or resentment …
A time when you were treated in a way you didn't want to be treated …
Maybe the person who made you feel that way apologized later …
    or maybe they didn't …
But you forgave them … because you understood … you were patient …
You knew that it was something you had to do … you wanted to do …
You offered someone forgiveness …
You offered your reconciliation …
To try to heal the wounds …
To heal the damage … to heal the hurt …

Now you and Jesus stand there and watch …
Watch yourself forgive them again … watch yourself heal them again …
And the Lord silently smiles … nods his head in approval …
Turns to you … anoints your forehead with his thumb … and smiles …
He holds you close with a hug …
Is there anything you would like to say to the Lord? …
Is there anything you would like to do? …

Jesus again invites you to another time in your life …
When you spent time with someone who was sad …
A time when you tried to comfort someone …
When you were a friend to someone in a difficult situation …
They were upset … and frustrated … and perhaps even crying …
And you stayed with them …
Close …
As a support …
Giving them strength … showing them that they were worth caring about …
Maybe it was a time when you didn't know what to say …
    but you could still just be with them …
As a friend … as someone who cared … as a sign of hope …
And you tried to help them …

Now … you stand there again … watching …
With Jesus next to you … together …
Hearing the words … clearly … watching the action … together …

The Lord silently smiles ... watching with an incredible wisdom
    that can see through you ... deeply into you ...
He turns to you ... anoints your forehead with his thumb ...
    and smiles ... nods his head in approval ...
And holds you close with a hug ...
Is there anything you would like to say to the Lord? ...
Is there anything you would like to do? ...

Jesus again invites you to another time ...
A time when you needed him very much ...
A time when you felt totally out of control or when you needed God's help ...
A time when you had to depend upon God ...
And you began to pray ...
Maybe for yourself ... maybe for someone else ...
Jesus takes you to this time when you felt you had to be close to God ...
That you couldn't do it without him ...
And quietly you tried to pray ... to surrender to God's will ...
To connect again with God in a special way ... giving God the freedom
    to take over ...
To create good from a difficult situation ...

Now you are there again ... once again ... at that special time ... watching ...
Just you and the Lord ... watching and listening quietly to your prayer ...
Listening to your heart pour out its needs to the Father in heaven ...
Just you and the Lord ... together ...
The Lord silently smiles ... knowing the feelings of your heart ...
Knowing your intense desire for him ...
He turns to you ... anoints your forehead with his thumb again ...
    and smiles ...
Nods his head in approval ...
And holds you close with a hug ...
Once more let yourself rest in the Lord's arms ...
Is there anything you would like to say to the Lord? ...
Is there anything you would like to do? ...

Jesus looks deeply into your eyes ... knowing all things about you ...
Things that even you haven't learned yet ...
He tells you that you were created ... at the very beginning ... by God ...
    in God's image ... in God's likeness ...
Jesus tells you that he was the original model you were created after ...
He is pleased ... and he is proud that you are slowly and gently becoming
    more and more like him ...

For the Lord looks into you and sees his very own ability to do things
    unselfishly for others …
His sacred ability to forgive … his strength to give comfort …
You even have his deep desire to be united with God in heaven …
    to connect with God in prayer …
And Jesus smiles … nodding his head in approval …
And holds you close with a hug …
Is there anything you would like to say to the Lord? …
Is there anything you would like to do? …

Again Jesus looks you directly in the eyes … knowing you …
And he gives you a new name …
Jesus whispers a new name to you that reflects all that you have done …
A new name that describes you … that describes the possibilities of who
    you are becoming …
A name that represents all that you are becoming in God's eyes …
And listen carefully … intently … as the Lord speaks your new name …
Your new name …
And Jesus asks you to become more and more like him …
He promises to help you … always …
He will be with you …
Always …

When you are ready … leave the Lord … and come back to this place …
    with your new name …
Given to you by God …
And know that you are not alone … there are others around you …
That care about you …
And be at peace …

When you are ready you may open your eyes …
But please remain still … quiet with everyone else …
To reflect for a few moments on all that the Lord has shown you …
On the new name that he has given to you …
And how you can become that name …
And be at peace …
Peace.

Meditation Fourteen

The Calming of the Storm

We learn to find a place of peace and quiet within ourselves, though storms may rage in our life. Inspired by Mark 4:35-41. The use of relaxation technique four is suggested. Time: 15 minutes

And we pray:
O glorious God ...
Who comforts and protects ...
Be merciful ...
Grant us your peace during this time of prayer ...
Help us to remain strong in you ...
As we face the storms in our lives ...
Knowing that your absolute love ...
Brings wonderful serenity and calm ...
Serenity and calm ...
Calm ...

With your eyes still closed ...
Look deep within yourself ...
Search the different feelings that drift within you ...
Bump into different feelings ...
Acknowledge them and then let them go ...
Keep searching ...
Maybe you are bumping into feelings of anxiety ...
That's alright ... let them go ...
Maybe you run into feelings of worry or anger ...
They cannot hurt you ...
Or control you ...
Let them go ...

Begin to look for a clearing ... deep within ...
Dismiss any kind of feeling that may be lingering ...
Just push it away ... allow it to evaporate ...
Go to that clearing deep within you ...
Alone ...

Now ... quietly ... gently ...
Call out the name of God ... softly call for Jesus ...

To be with you …
Together …
With nothing else …
The two of you together …
Watch the way Jesus greets you …
Listen to what he says …
See what he does …
Is there anything you want to say to the Lord? …
Anything you want to do? …

Let Jesus take you by the hand …
Let him ever so carefully bring you to a very large sea …
You can hear the water lapping against the shore …
Feel the cool breeze drifting over the water surface …
Making small dimpled waves that glide over the water …
Breathe in the smell of a huge lake that seems as wide as the ocean …
Jesus points along the horizon to a fishing boat …
    out in the middle of the lake …
Where he will take you … across the water … as if you were weightless …
    slowly walking to the fishing boat …

In the distance … you can see the sky turning grey … growing darker …
And across the expanse of the lake … the storm clouds gather and
    slowly move …
Blackness slowly sweeps across the water …
You can faintly hear the echo of thunder … a rumble in the distance …
Moving in … drawing closer to the boat of people that you approach
    with the Lord …
You can see the waves growing … rougher … stronger …
The wind blows against the waves … against the whitecaps …
    spraying water in the air … spraying chilly water against you …
The warmth of the sun has been covered by the storm … it is gone …
The spray of the water is cold … and raw …
Lightning crackles against the water … dances through the furious billowing
    of the waves …

You come still closer to the fishing boat filled with people …
The storm is lifting the water … splashing the water … twisting the water …
    slamming it against the boat … into the boat …
Crashing thunder surrounds you …
You can see the faces of the people in the boat clearly …
Listen to their panic … their fear …

Hear what they are saying ... what are they crying out for? ...
    what do they need? ...
And what are the feelings inside you? ... How do you react? ...
How do you feel for them? ... for yourself? ...
You can feel the strength of Jesus holding your hand ...
Standing with you ... you know he would never allow anything
    to harm or hurt you ...
There is strength in the Lord's hand ...
Is there anything you want to say to the Lord? ...
Anything you would like to do? ...

Jesus raises his arms ... lifting them to heaven ... stretching them out
    with confidence ... with power ...
And with total control, Jesus softly ... gently says ...
Quiet ... Be still ...
Be still ...
Hush ...

The warmth of the new sun dissolves the storm clouds ... but only in this
    area of the sea ... in this single place of brightness ...
Only here the water slows to a gentle roll ...
Slightly lapping against the boat ...
Only here the sun sparkles ... dancing over the water surface ...
While all around the storm still rages ...
Only here is it quiet ... peaceful ... tranquil ... while you can still see a
    terrible storm twist and splash around you ...
This small area is protected ... filled with the Lord's presence ... and peace ...
And it is quiet ... and hushed ...
Still ...
And hushed ...

Look again at the people in the fishing boat ... what are they saying? ...
    what are they doing? ...
Is there anything you want to say to the Lord? ...
Is there anything you want to do? ...
Be at peace in this protected place ...
Be still ...
Calm ...

Jesus takes you in his arms ...
And holds you close ...
You can feel the power of his peace ...

Being held in the calm of his presence …
At peace …

And the sea … and the storm … and the boat … and the water … disappear …
You find yourself moving back … deep within to the clearing where Jesus
    first came to you … with the same calmness … tranquility … stillness …
Alone … with no feelings to distract you …
Just you and the Lord …
Together …
Deep within you …

Jesus asks if there was a time in your life when it felt like a storm was raging
    around you? …
A time when you felt out of control …
Was there a time of great noise and hurting? …
Maybe of yelling and pain …

Jesus asks you to take him by the hand …
He asks you to take him to that time …
Take him to that place where there was hurting …
Where there was anger …
Noise and commotion … maybe fists … shouting …
Like an enormous storm that unexpectedly exploded …
The fury of a huge storm unfurled …
A time when you felt hopeless … tossed and turned like a tiny boat
    in a huge storm …
Jesus asks you to take him to that time and place …
By his hand … take Jesus to that incident … and just stand and watch …
Separate … but in the midst …
Listen and watch …
Listen to the noise … the screeching … the arguing … the energy …
    the power …
Watch the gathering of force …
Watch the anger … the confusion … the pain …
Like a raging storm out of control …
Out of control …

What are the feelings inside of you …
What is happening inside you …
Tell the Lord what it feels like …
Slowly … gently … try to explain …
So that God … the Lord … can feel the same thing with you …
So that he can share in the storm in your life …

Together ...
Share the hurt ... the confusion ...
Maybe regret ... maybe anger ... maybe betrayal ...
Maybe humiliation ... or rejection ... or loneliness ...
Together ... you and the Lord ...
Jesus knows the feelings ... the storm ... and it has become part of him
    as well ...
Uniting both of you ... together ... united in this storm ...
Is there anything you want to say to the Lord? ...
Anything you want to do? ...

Jesus takes you back again to the time of hurt ... the scene ...
    that was like a storm ...
And he asks you to see it in a new way ...
To look at the people with his eyes ...
To share in his vision ...
The Lord gently waves his hand ... so you can see inside each of the people ...
See inside the people there ... see their feelings clearly ... look inside them ...
See the feelings that are making this storm happen ...
Jesus points to each of their feelings ... so that you see them the way the Lord
    sees them ...
All the feelings of everyone ...
Their fear ... their anxiety ... their worry ...
The fear they hold on to tightly ... because they want to be in total control ...
    because they are afraid and can't let go ...
Their frustration ... their envy and jealousy ... of you ...
Their fear ...

You can feel the strength of Jesus holding your hand ...
Standing with you ... you knew he would never allow anything
    to harm you ...
You can feel the strength of the Lord's hand ...
Jesus raises his arms ... lifting them to heaven ... stretching them out
    with confidence ... with power ...
With total control Jesus softly ... gently says ...
Quiet ... Be still ...
Be still ...
Hush ...

You can sense each of those feelings inside of you becoming smooth ...
Each feeling becoming calm ... still ... at peace ...
Peace ...

No matter how strong or powerful that storm was ... there is now a calm ...
    a sense of peace ...
There is understanding ... patience ...
Jesus holds you close to himself ...
You can feel his protection ...
The Lord asks you if there is anything you want to say to those people ...
With the Lord's strength ...
Is there anything you want to tell them? ...
Anything you want to do? ...

The Lord holds you close to his heart ...
Deep within his arms ...
He will never let go of you ...
Be at peace ...
At peace ...

Now Jesus takes you back to that clearing deep within you ...
That place where you can be alone with God ...
And Jesus brings a brightness ... he brings a powerful calm ...
    to this clearing deep within you ...
Jesus promises that here ... it can always be calm ... peaceful ...
    here you can always ... forever ... find him ...
Here you can always find a protected place of calm ...
In any storm ...
A source of strength and peace that can bring calm to any storm ...
Know the promise of the Lord ... his protected place of peace ...
    deep within you ...
Protected ... within you ... forever ...

With that place of calm still deep within you ... alive and real ...
Know that God's calm and peace will always be within you ...
Calm to control the storms ...
Peace to heal the hurts and fears ...
Bring back with you the peace and the calm of the Lord ...
When you are ready ... come back ... knowing that you are not alone
There are others here who also need the peace and calm that you
    bring back with you ...
Peace that you can share ...
When you are ready ... you may open your eyes ...
Be at peace ...
Never lose that protected place ... the clearing of calm and peace within you ...
Be at peace ...
At peace.

Meditation Fifteen

Feeding of the Five Thousand

We discover the power of sharing, as we gain confidence in having enough.
Inspired by John 6:1-13. The use of relaxation technique two is suggested.
Time: 12 minutes

And we pray:
All-loving and generous God …
You long for us to learn from you …
To learn your ways and your desires for us …
And we want to …
We want to live up to your expectations of us …
But we are often distracted …
We become preoccupied by everyday needs … worries … fears … jealousies …
So help us today … during our prayer … to discover in our lives …
Your will … your way … your generosity …
So that we might be free to learn eagerly from you …

With your eyes still closed …
Take a slow … and silent deep breath …
Hold it for a few seconds …
As you release that breath …
Let it propel you to a very peaceful knoll …
To the top of a small hill … covered by lush grass …
Damp and thick … soft like a cushion …
The carpet of grass smells fresh … like there's been a soft rain …
    bringing everything to life …
Just settle down and sit on the top of the mount … alone … safe …
With an incredible view … stretching into a valley …
    gentle breezes tipping the edges of grass …
In waves … blowing softly …
You can see a few birds gliding and dipping … weaving lazy loops
    through the sky …
Listen carefully to the silence … like a silent song of perfect harmony …
What do you hear? … this is God's song … what is the sound? …
And be at peace …

Look down the slope … and across the fields … beyond the
    edge of the world …

111

What do you see? … this creation of God … what is the view? …
And be at peace …
Feel the grass around you … thick and soft … growing … alive …
    its very soul beneath you …
What do you feel? … this life is of God … what is it like to your touch? …
And be at peace …
In the safety of God's kingdom …
Be at peace …
Peace …

With your eyes closed …
Take a deep breath …
And slowly … silently exhale …
With that breath several people appear … sitting together …
    clustered on the mount … on the grass …
Several people that you remember … people who have touched your life …
    who have helped you … supported you …
People who were there for you when you needed them …
Looking at you, they remember that time … and they nod in approval …

Now take another breath …
Deeply … silently …
And as you slowly exhale … another cluster of people appear who have
    touched you with love …
People you remember helping you … people who have given to you …
    have shared with you … have been there for you …
They too sit in a small cluster … on the lawn … on the side of the mount …

Slowly … with another breath … more people gather …
All sitting in small clusters around the mount …
People who have been important to you …
Family … friends … people you have worked with …
People you have learned with … and have learned from …
Some people very familiar … others that you have seen or known
    only briefly …
People that you may have forgotten … but still … were important
    at some time in your life …
All gathering around you … sitting on the grass … people who have
    touched your life …
Have touched your heart …

Now suddenly you feel as though someone has approached you …
    on top of that knoll …

You are aware of someone behind you ... someone you had not noticed ...
   but who may have been there all the time ...
Silently ... patiently ... just there ... and never noticed ...
Don't turn around ... don't look ...
Just feel the person ...
Feel his friendship ... his concern ... his devotion to you ...
Always working for you ... invisibly caring ... silently helping ...

You can feel his hand ... slowly slide along your shoulder ... to hold you
   to connect with you ...
His arm ... loving you ... across your shoulders to hug you ...
   to let you know how much he loves you ...
You can feel his protection ...
Be at peace in the arms of God ...
In the arms of Jesus who has been watching over you ... with all these people
   gathered together on the mount ... gathered together around you ...
Is there anything you would like to say to Jesus? ...
Is there anything you would like to do? ...
And be at peace ...

Jesus asks you to remember ... to go back in your memory to another time ...
   a time when you were overwhelmed by a task ...
When you knew that you had a project that had to be accomplished ...
A time when you were reluctant or afraid because of something that
   seemed to overwhelm you ...
A task or project ... that seemed too big ... and the expectations seemed
   enormous ... and the pressure to accomplish seemed overwhelming ...

Invite the Lord to explore that memory with you ...
To feel the feelings of that event ...
You are there again with the Lord ...
Together ...
Jesus touches your eyes ... and you see the project completed ... finished ...
   and sense the feeling of being satisfied ...
Accomplishment ...
In spite of the fear ... in spite of the dread ...
Accomplishment ...
Did you do it alone? ...
Perhaps someone came to your aid ...
To encourage ... to simplify things ... to help you ...
If someone was there for you ... find them on the lawn ... go to them ...
   and take Jesus with you ...

113

Is there anything you would like to say to them? ...
Anything you would like to do? ...

The Lord thanks them for letting him use them ... in order to help you ...
Jesus helped take care of the situation in his own unique way ...
Better than you ever thought possible ...
More wonderfully than you could have ever expected ...
In his generosity ... God gave you all that was necessary ... and even more ...
The Lord touches your forehead ... and speaks of confidence ...
Confidence in his generosity ...
Is there anything you would like to say to him? ...
Is there anything you would like to do?
And be at peace ...
Peace.

The Lord asks you once more to remember another time ...
When God brought a special person into your life to help you ...
When you didn't think that you were going to make it ...
Perhaps you were overwhelmed ... or lonely ... or felt forgotten ...
But the Lord brought someone into your life ...
Maybe it was just as you were about to give up ... to let go ... or fail ...
That other person came into your life ...
So unexpectedly ...
So timely ... a gift from God ...
They helped you during that time ...
They assured you ... gave you a new reason to push on ...
    to hold on to the situation ...
And together ... it seemed to come together ... to make sense ... to work out ...
You had great energy ... stamina ... and you accomplished ...
    more than you ever thought possible ...
That person gave you what you needed ... and more ...
Beyond your every dream ...

Go find that person ... find them in the crowd on the lawn ...
    sitting in the grass ... patiently resting on the hill ...
    trusting in the power of God ...
They sit there ... resting with God ...
Find them ... and go to them ...
Is there anything you would like to say to them? ...
Is there anything you would like to do? ...
Rest with them ...
Patiently ...

Jesus is there with you ... and he thanks them ... gratefully ...
    that they let him work through them ...
That he was able to provide for you ... more than you could ever expect ...
    through them ...
Jesus gives them a great big hug ...
And be at peace ...
Peace ...

And the Lord touches your forehead again ... anointing you ...
    and speaking his word ... a word of confidence ...
Like a prayer ... for you ...
A prayer of confidence ... for you ...
Jesus promises that he will always take care of you ... because of his great love
    for you ... his great devotion to you ...

You stand on the hill again with the Lord beside you ...
He extends his arm before you ... gesturing to all the people who have
    gathered before you ... who are resting with the Lord ... around the hill ...
Jesus tells you that these are the people that are willing to share what he has
    given to them with you ...
Those who willingly show the Lord's devotion to you ...
His people ...
You can feel the power of their trust ... collectively ... the power of their
    sharing to do the impossible ...
You can feel their incredible love ... for you ... from God ... to you ...
And their desire to share ... because the Lord has provided so much
    for them ...
More than enough ... of what really matters ... of what God knows
    is truly important ...
Is there anything you would like to say to the Lord? ...
Is there anything you would like to do? ...

Jesus tells you how much he has provided for you ... and the abundance
    that he has given to you ...
He tells you about his desire for you to join these people ...
    his people on the lawn ... these people who are willing to share ...
    and give of themselves to others ...
Because the Lord has prayed for your confidence ... has given to you his
    confidence ... in having enough ...
Is there anything you would like to say to the Lord? ...
Is there anything you would like to do?
And be at peace ...
At peace ...

When you are ready ... you may leave the mount ... leave the people
    that have been so good to you ...
And you can return here ...
Know that you are not alone ... there are others who are here with you ...
Who care about you ...
Others here who have joined God's people ...
In the confidence of sharing ...

When you are ready ... you may open your eyes ...
But please remain still ...
Remain quiet ...
Just reflect for a few minutes ...
Remember all the times that the Lord has provided for you so generously ...
So that you may provide for others ...
Be confident of God ...
And at peace ...
Peace.

Meditation Sixteen

The Raising of Lazarus

We are freed from that which binds us: self-judgment, feelings of inadequacy, fears, anger, and resentment. Inspired by John 11:1-44. The use of relaxation technique four is suggested. Time: 15 minutes

And we pray:
God of life and promise …
You continually breathe new life into that which seems burdened and lifeless …
Reawakening with your Spirit …
A promise of victory …
Hope inflamed …
Send that same Spirit to us as we meditate …
That we too may regain what we've lost …
And rejoice in the power of your reviving and healing love …

With your eyes still closed …
Take a journey …
To a place where you have never been before …
Take a journey … by yourself … to a place that is dark …
Where you can't see anything around you …
Only what seems like miles and miles of darkness …
A place where you are alone … and yet safe … very safe …
There is nothing there that can harm you …
The total darkness even seems to make it safer …
Just be there alone …
Alone …

In the darkness …
Touch the floor with your hand …
You can't see it … but you can feel it …
Is it hard like concrete … or wood …
Or is it softer … like dirt … firm earth? …
Very solid and safe … in the darkness …
Breathe in the air … stale air … not fresh at all … maybe even musty …
Like a deep earthy forest …
It is damp … cool … the air feels like a cold sweat … clammy …
And it is dark …

Now slowly reach to the side … stretch out your arms and hands …
    to feel if there is anything there …
Firmness … a wall … solid … it too is cool and damp …
Follow it around … until you find a corner … and continue …
    until you reach another corner …
An enclosed area … of darkness …
As you follow the walls … feeling along them … hands outstretched …
You feel something different … harder … colder … like a giant rock …
    that stands up in front of you …
Irregular … rough … and cool …
You feel that you are sealed into this area …
But you are safe … and nothing will harm you …

Then … from behind you … a voice …
A comforting voice … soothing and confident … a voice that reassures you
    that everything is alright … and there is nothing to worry you …
You can hear someone strike a match … that glows … softly …
A small fire starts … that brings light … and warmth …
    it flickers … chasing away the fears …
Now you can see the face … of the person who was talking …
It is someone you know who has been close to the Lord …
Someone who has been a close friend to Jesus …
Someone who looks like a friend of yours … that has had a close friendship
    with the Lord …
They want to be with you …
So you are not alone …
So they can give comfort … and help …
Is there anything you would like to say to this person? …
Anything you would like to do? …

This person tells you that you are in a cave …
And that it's really not so bad … as a matter of fact … there is safety here …
    no one can get to you … you can feel secure …
It can be lonely, of course … but that's why you both are here … together …
And be at peace …
At peace …

The person tells you that there was a doorway … an opening …
    there used to be a doorway …
But it's blocked now …
Sealed … to make it a safer place …

And they point to the wall that seemed to be a large stone
    standing up in front of you ...
In the flickering light from the fire ... you can see clearly ...
It's not just one stone ... but a whole series of stones ... in front of each other ...
    on top of each other ... but securely keeping you safe ... in your cave ...
You ask about the fire ... because there is no more wood ... and you know that
    the light can only last for a little while ... and you fear that the friend might
    leave with the light ... and then it will be damp ... and dark ... and cool ...
    and you'll be all alone ...
Is there anything you want to say to your friend? ...
Is there anything you want to do? ...

Your friend says that the stones can be removed ... but it's not easy ...
    perhaps there will be light outside if you can just move the stones ...
You try to budge a big one in front of you ... the one that is closest ...
You can feel your muscles strain ... but the stone doesn't move ... not a hair ...
Your friend suggests trying the farthest stone first ... the one that is closest to
    the outside ... furthest from you ... one you can't even reach ...
That idea seems stupid ... futile ... because you know you could never get
    at it ... let alone move it ...
But your friend says that all you need is a glimpse of it ...
You just need to recognize it ... name it ... and then you'll be able to
    control it ... to move it ... or even to destroy it ...
If you want to get out ... as the light flickers away into the darkness of the cave ...
    you have to try to move that stone ...
So you try to see the furthest rock ... there are letters scribbled on it ...
    letters that you can barely make out ... s ... e ... l ... f ... j ... u ... d ... g ...
    m ... e ... n ... t ...
Self-judgment ...

Your friend asks you what it means ...
And wonders if maybe it has to do with those times ... or those ways ...
    that you have judged yourself ... critically ...
Judged yourself too critically ...
Your friend asks if you have ever been too critical of yourself ...
When? ... How? ...
Have you put yourself down ... or mocked yourself? ...

Perhaps you remember a time when you thought you failed to live up to
    being perfect ...
And you wanted to punish yourself in some way ...

With great trust … help this new friend to understand what the word
   on that rock could be referring to …
Take the time to explain …
Be at peace … and very trusting …
Trusting …

As you explain one of those times that you have been too critical of yourself …
   you hear the deep rattle and rumble … of that stone rolling away …
You can see the faint brightness of light coming from that small opening …
With that light it is easier to see something inscribed on the next stone …
   the one in the back … you can see the words …
And you squint to try to read them …
You can see the words Feelings of Inadequacy …

Your friend thinks that those must have come because of judging yourself
   so critically …
And your friend asks about those feelings of inadequacy …
Explain to your friend what those feelings are like … so that you can get rid
   of them …
Think of a time in your life recently when you have felt inadequate …
   perhaps you didn't reach your own expectations …
Perhaps you felt like you should give up because you thought someone else
   was better …

Again … as you share you feelings … you can hear the same deep rumbling of
   another rock rolling away …
And a beam of light comes into the cave as the fire goes out …
But the opening is too high and you can't look out …
You can only see the bright beam of light cutting through the darkness …
   bouncing off the back wall …
As you look … you can see another inscription on the rock that is now the
   furthest away …
And the rock is marked with the inscription Fear …

Stop for a minute to reflect about what fear has been keeping you locked away
   … keeping you in this dark, safe place …
Think of a recent fear that you've had … of something that you dread …
   or worry about …
Something that might preoccupy you with worry …
A fear that makes you want to seek a safe place where nothing can reach you …
A fear that can freeze you … or keep you from being free …

Softly ... gently ... confide this fear to the friend that remains ...
    to comfort you ... to support and help you ...
It's not easy to share the fear ... but as you do ... the next stone
    rumbles away also ...
You can hear the huge, heavy rock ... leave you ...

And the room is getting brighter now ...
Bright enough to see the next stone and the two words inscribed on it ...
    the words Anger and Resentment ....
You know that you need to try to remember what has made you the
    most angry ...
What has filled you with the most resentment? ...
What has blinded you with the darkness of anger? ...
Blotting out anything that could have made you happy ...
What has most recently brought you the bitterness of anger? ...
Made you feel so very heavy with resentment? ...
Let it go ... give it away ... share it with your friend ... who understands ...
    who can bring you the healing love of God ...
Just let go of it ... and be free ...
Free ...

Now that rock has been pushed away ... and the light has gotten brighter ...
    there is one last rock that keeps you from leaving ... from walking out into
    the freshness of new life ...
And the rock that remains ... the one that still blocks the way ...
    is labeled with the word Stubbornness ...

The result of the self-judgment and feelings of inadequacy ... the fears ...
    and the anger which festered and became resentment within you ...
It is this last stone called stubbornness ... that has helped to protect you ...
    but has kept you from real freedom ...
To finally be free ... you must think about stubbornness ...
Times when you were demanding and too determined ... maybe it was
    a way of getting even ... or proving that you were right and everyone else
    was wrong ...
A time when your anger became a wall of distance ... an artificial strength ...
    that kept the people away ... that kept the living away ... and protected
    you with loneliness ...
Now with your new freedom from fear ... and from anger ...
    and from all that self-criticism ...
You know you really don't need the stubbornness ... that it won't help you
    anymore ... that there is nothing that it can protect you from ...

You can let go ... hand it over to your friend ... and watch the last big stone
   roll slowly away and disappear ...

The doorway is open now ... and the warm sun glows throughout your cave ...
   you can see now that it was like a tomb ... a place for the dead ...
   a place you no longer need ...
The warmth of the bright day invites you to come out into the beauty of an
   incredible new world ...
You walk with a new feeling of being light ... like the air ...
   walking on a breeze that supports you ...
As you walk from the tomb ...
A person stands before you ... with arms wide ... welcoming you ...
   celebrating your new freedom ...
And as you come closer to this person ...
Their face seems to resemble the face of your friend ...
Who was with you in the tomb ...
But you know that this is the Lord ...
Your God who has been caring for you ...
Inviting you to new freedom ...
The one who has been rolling away the stones that kept you separated from
   the living ...
Your God ... who welcomes you to new life ... and wraps gentle arms
   around you ...
You can feel the strength of new life come into you ... a new life that fills you ...
Just rest now with your God ... in peace ...
Peace ...

When you are ready ...
Leave that place and return here ...
But bring back with you that lightness ... that new life ...
The new strength of God ... that will never leave you ...
And be at peace ...
Peace ...

When you are ready to open your eyes ...
Don't look at anyone ... or talk to anyone ...
Just reflect quietly on the experience of new life ...
   the experience of being made free ...
And know that it remains ...
Know that it can never be taken from you ...
And be at peace ...
Peace.

Meditation Seventeen

Gathering for the Lord's Last Supper

Experiencing the inherent power of Christ's gift of his body and blood, we partake of the final meal, we recognize people from our own lives gathered with us, and we see the impact of our communion with each other and with Christ. Inspired by Luke 22:7-23. The use of relaxation technique three is suggested. Time: 14 minutes

And we pray:
God of the Covenant …
Almighty Father of unbreakable promises …
You forever gather people into a family …
Bringing us into union with you and binding us together …
That you may speak to us your word of fidelity …
As we meditate this day …
Grant us your Holy Spirit … that we may enter into and experience …
    your ultimate meal … your ultimate promise of eternal life …
Foreshadowing your ultimate sacrifice …
Which purifies us of all our faults … of all our sins …
That we may be holy … in your sight … forever …

With your eyes still closed …
Travel to another time …
Travel to another place …
Far away … to ancient Jerusalem …
Many centuries ago …
To a city tucked within high protective walls … built of hard mud bricks …
    atop a parched hill …
A large city … filled with talking people … and noisy animals …
    and beasts of burden …
Breathe in the exotic smells of spices cooking … and fresh fish and
    vegetables … and smoldering fires …
Push through the narrow streets … framed with bolts of bright fabrics …
    colors hanging from windows … children running and playing …
    a small cluster of goats …

Up ahead … you can see your destination … a high tower … surrounded by a
    complex of large square buildings … a citadel …

123

Finally you are there at the citadel ... you find a doorway ... a small
    doorway ... and you have to stoop a little to enter ...
There are stairs to climb ... steep and slow ... up and up until you're
    short of breath ...
And then you're at the top ...

Around a corner ... you can hear singing ... a group slowly chanting ...
When they stop ... laughter breaks out ... and you see them all point to the
    one on the end ... who can't sing very well ... who throws everyone off ...
But you know that they still enjoy each other ... and that they are
    close friends ...
They all are sitting or lying on the floor ... spread out around a low table
    which is set with flat bread ... and greens ... a roast ... and eggs ...
    mixtures of condiments ... goblets for wine ...
Looking carefully at their faces you recognize the one at the end ...
    stretched out ... propped up on one elbow ... that face ... the smile ...
    the welcoming gesture ...
Jesus beckons you with his hand ... to join them ... to share this special meal ...

There's a kind of somberness among the group ... it's a celebration ...
    but a quiet celebration ... they are reflective ...
You join the Lord as he puts his finger to his lips ... a hush which announces
    an important story ...
The youngest there asks why this night is so important ...
    and the story unfolds ...
A story about leaving slavery ... and oppression ...
Leaving that which held us captive ...
And a miraculous deliverance ... making us free ...
Free with new life that is beyond anything we could ever dream of ...
On this day we remember ... we remember the story ... we make it
    real once more ... keeping it alive ... rendering it eternal ...
Everyone sips the wine ... sharing in the memory ... accepting the story ...
    pledging together that it is their story as well ...

You realize suddenly that there is no cup for you ...
And Jesus realizes this too ...
So he lifts his own cup to you ... but then he pulls it back before letting you
    sip from it ...
And he speaks ... a hushed murmur ... yet everyone hears him ...
    the cup he says ... is to be divided among all ... to be shared by all ...
He lifts the piece of broken bread ... edges crushed ... the sustenance of life ...
    the source of daily strength ... bread ... broken ... and shared ...

Jesus identifies himself with this bread ... a source of new life ... a source of
    new freedom from slavery ... deliverance ...
This bread broken ... like his life will be broken ... so that others might
    be mended ...
With divine power ... with divine life ... the new food from heaven ...
    offered to you ...
Jesus identifies with the cup ... a pledge ... a promise ... a covenant ...
Sealed with life ... God's life ... a promise sealed in God's blood ...
    so that it can never be broken ... eternal ...
Is there anything you would like to say to the Lord? ...
Is there anything you would like to do? ...

Look around you again at the people gathered for the meal ... the faces of the
    people around the table ... are beginning to change ...
They start to resemble different people ... people that you know ...
    people with whom you have shared your life ...
Now you recognize someone who sits near you ... someone who loves you
    very much ...
Someone who has been unselfish ... who has cared for you deeply ...
    even when you weren't aware of it ...
They sit at the table with you ... someone who is very devoted to you ...
    who has pledged their love ... perhaps in silence ... perhaps in words
    spoken between you ...
And Jesus thanks that person ... for loving you so much ... and offers them
    the cup and the bread ...
Is there anything you would like to say to them? ...
Anything you would like to do? ...

The Lord offers you the cup and bread as well ... sealing the union
    between you and this person who loves you so much ...
Think about how their love may have given you the freedom to be yourself ...
    without any masks ...
How it may have opened your eyes to an exhilarating new life ...
How their love may have given you the strength to face whatever might
    come along ...
Is there anything you would like to tell the Lord? ...
Is there anything you would like to do? ...
And be at peace ...

Look around the table again ... this time you notice someone you know that
    doesn't have much confidence in you ...
Perhaps someone who often discourages you ...

A person who doesn't trust you as much as you would like them to …
Who doesn't have much faith in you …
Jesus asks you … what would you like them to say to you? …
    what do you think that they would say? …
Listen … listen carefully …
How can you come to an understanding with this person? …
How might you change things to help them trust you? …
What could make it better? …
Is there anything you would like to say to that person whom you feel
    has so little faith in you? …
The Lord offers both of you his bread of new life … and the cup of salvation …
    the cup of forgiveness …
As a union between you …
And be at peace …
In understanding and harmony …

Looking around the table once more … you recognize another face …
    the face of a person who often tries to convince you of their way …
A person who may try to push you into things you really don't want to do …
Someone who seems always to want to do things their own way …
Which sometimes makes things very difficult …
Go to them … sit with them … talk with them …
What would you like them to say? …
What do you think their words would be? …
Be with them … comfortably … patiently …
Help them to understand your feelings …
Is there anything you would like to say to them? …
Is there anything you would like to do? …

Again Jesus offers both of you the bread and the wine … together …
    the bread which he holds in communion … to bind together … to heal …
    to unite …
And the cup of understanding … the cup of his pledge and commitment …
    the cup of promise …
He brings it to both of you …
To hold you in union …
Once more be at peace …

As you look around the table once again …
You notice a familiar face trying to hide from you …
Trying to duck behind the others … so that you won't notice them …
But you do … and you recognize a person who has betrayed you …

126

A person who has done to you what you never thought that they would ...
Someone who has broken their commitment ... their pledge ...
A person who has disappointed you ...
And has left you feeling hurt ...

Now Jesus senses that something is wrong with you ...
He turns to see who you are looking at ... and he understands ... the pain ...
    the frustration ... the betrayal ...
And he comes to you ...
Puts his arms over your shoulders ...
And tells you that it is alright ...
He has been betrayed as well ... many times ... by many different people ...
Is there anything you want to explain to the Lord? ...
Anything you would like to do? ...

Listen carefully to what Jesus says to you ... what is his reply? ...
And be at peace ...
Peace ...

The person at the table who loves you the most ... comes to your side ...
And offers you the cup of forgiveness ... offers you understanding and
    acceptance ... the bread of new freedom ... the bread of new life ...
You can be confident that Jesus will never leave you ... never betray you ...
    never push you away ... never lose faith or confidence in you ...
You can be sure that he offers you his bread of eternal life ...
    his cup of eternal salvation ...
And as you eat ... and as you drink ... a bond develops and grows ...
You can feel the power of Christ ... energizing you ... filling you with
    freedom ... melting the masks and lies that others would live behind ...
You can feel the energy of God that holds you close like a magnet ...
    giving you new confidence and faith ...
Again be at peace ...
Be free ... in union with God ...
Sharing a mutual life ...
And be at peace ...
Peace ...

When you are ready ...
Leave that table ... and the people you know ...
Leave the room that was up those steep stairs ...
Leave Jerusalem and the noisy, narrow streets ...
And come back here ...

Return to this room …
And know that you are still not alone …
There are others who are here …
Others who also know the transforming power of the Last Supper …

When you are ready … you may slowly, peacefully open your eyes …
But please don't try to talk to anyone …
Or distract them …
Just privately remember the meal that you just shared with the Lord …
    remember to keep it real …
Remember how it can transform …
And make new …
And bring peace …
Peace.

Christ's Final Prayer for Unity

We discover the Christ that comes to us in the many people with whom we share our lives. It is the Christ-with-others that unites us in his sacrament. Inspired by John 17:20-23. The use of relaxation technique one is suggested. Time: 11 minutes

And we pray:
Lord Jesus Christ ...
Be with us as we meditate ...
Send your Holy Spirit ... your Spirit of peace ...
Guide us in our prayer ...
Take away any fear ... for we trust in you ...
Help us to see you ... and feel you ...
To recognize you in the people you send to us ...
Be with us Lord, guide us with peace ...
Stay near ...

With your eyes closed ... travel in your imagination to a very safe place ...
To a place that you know ... that you are familiar with ...
To a place where you feel that you belong ...
Where no one can hurt you ...
Where you feel very comfortable ... very safe ...
Is it warm there? ... or is it cool? ...
Is it bright? ... or is it dark? ...
Can you smell anything? ...
Look around and see all the different things around you ...
What is in this special place? ...
Memories? ... your favorite things? ...
Just be at peace ...
Peace ...

Realize that you are not alone ...
From behind ...
Someone is walking toward you ... slowly ...
You can't see who it is ... but that's alright ...
Don't turn around ... don't look ... just feel someone gently approaching ...
    from behind you ...
You can feel security in their friendship ... as they come closer to you ...
    from behind ...

You feel overwhelming forgiveness as they slowly approach ...
And deep understanding ... something you wish for ... but rarely find ...
    the deepest understanding ...
You can sense someone is standing behind you ... closely ... silently ...
You can feel the warmth of their love ...
An incredible love ... that can bring peace ...

And you can feel a hand on your shoulder ...
You can't see anyone ... but you can feel a hand ... a strong hand yet gentle ...
    firm yet comforting ...
Slowly ... you turn around ...
You feel the hand slide across your shoulders ...
And you look up ... and see the smiling face of Jesus ...
He draws you close to himself ...
Wraps his arms around you ...
Giving you a warm hug ...
He draws your face to his chest ... gently ...
You can hear his heart beat ... so strong ...
And you can feel his deep love ... God's love ...
Is there anything you would like to say to the Lord? ...
Is there anything you would like to do? ...

Now as you pull back ... Jesus asks if he can invite someone else to join
    both of you ...
And he calls out the name of your best friend ...
And ... suddenly ... the three of you are standing there ... you ... Jesus ...
    and your best friend ...
And Jesus thanks your friend for being so faithful to you ... for being there for
    you when you need them ...
He thanks your best friend for all the good times that you shared ...
    and for looking out for you ... for helping ...
Then the Lord goes to your best friend and gives them a great big hug ...
    in gratitude ...
Is there anything you want to say to your best friend? ...
Is there anything you want to do? ...
Be at peace ...

Now the Lord calls out the name of your favorite relative ...
Think of all the people in your family ... your aunts ... uncles ... cousins ...
    brothers and sisters ... grandparents ... parents ...
The Lord calls out the name of the one person in your family that is the most
    special to you ...

The one that you will never forget ... that gives you so many great memories ...
The one special relative that makes you feel so special ...

And now ... all of you ... are standing there together ...
Your favorite relative, your best friend, you and the Lord ...
And the Lord goes to your favorite relative and thanks them for
     having loved you so much ...
For having taken such good care of you ... for being concerned and caring ...
For being so lovable ...
And the Lord gives them a great big hug and his love ...
Is there anything you want to say to your favorite relative? ...
Anything you would like to do? ...

The Lord now calls out the name of your favorite teacher ...
Of all the different teachers that you have ever had ... over so many years ...
The Lord now calls out the name of your favorite teacher ...
The one teacher that was so special ... that you will never forget them ... ever ...
One special person that taught you so much ... and had such a great impact
     on your life ...
And now ... you stand there with your best friend, your favorite relative,
     your favorite teacher, you, and the Lord ...
And the Lord goes to that teacher and thanks them for giving you
     so much time ... for giving you so much special attention ...
Jesus thanks them for having such confidence in you ... for being so patient
     with you ... and so understanding ...
The Lord goes to them ... thanks them for all their patience and dedication ...
And gives them a great big hug ...
Is there anything you want to say to your teacher? ...
Anything you want to do? ...

Again the Lord calls out a name you recognize ...
The Lord calls out the name of a person from school that everyone laughs at ...
A person that people make fun of ...
A person that is the brunt of everybody's jokes ...
Someone who has no friends ... and is usually alone ...
Someone no one else understands ... that no one wants to include ...
There you all are together ... your best friend ... your favorite relative ...
     your teacher ... and the person that everyone makes fun of ...
     with you and the Lord ...
And Jesus goes to that person ... and apologizes for everyone else ...

He tells them that he understands … people laughed at him as well …
    and mocked him, too …
Then he gently gives that person a big hug …

The Lord waves his hand in front of the person that everyone puts down …
    and laughs at …
And you can suddenly see inside them …
You can see all the scars from all the laughter and all the jokes …
You can see all the pain from the rejection they felt and from their loneliness …
You can see the marks of all the hurt and all the suffering that others have
    inflicted on them …
And the Lord holds them in his arms …
And tells them how much he loves them …
And asks them for their forgiveness … he asks them to forgive everyone who
    has laughed at them … who has hurt them …
Is there anything you want to say? …
Anything you want to do? …

One last time the Lord calls out a name …
This time he calls a person who has really hurt you …
Who is he calling? … What name do you hear? …
It is a person who has treated you in a way that angered you …
Someone who has betrayed you or has talked badly about you …
Someone who may have disappointed you … or caused you regret and
    frustration …
So now everyone stands together … your best friend … your favorite relative …
    a special teacher … the person everyone laughed at … and now the person
    that has treated you in a way you didn't want to be treated …
    with you and the Lord …

And the Lord goes to that person … who treated you poorly …
And he waves his hand in front of them, and again, you can see inside them …
You can see the scars from all their anger … and the put-downs …
You can see the incredible rejection that they have felt in their life too …
The anger they have from not being the best …
But look closely … you can see something you never expected …
You can see the marks within them of the jealousy they have …
Jealousy that has eaten away at them …
Jealousy … of you …
You can see how much they have envied you …
And wished that they could be like you …

How they wished that they had what you had ... and could do the things that
  you can do ... and have the friends that you have ...
You can see it was all the jealousy that has caused them to hurt you ...
Now the Lord takes their hand and puts it into yours ...
And holds them both together ... with his ...
And the Lord asks you if you can forgive ... as he has forgiven ...
Is there anything you want to say to them? ...
Is there anything you would like to do? ...

And the Lord puts all of you into a large circle ...
You ... with your best friend ... and your favorite relative ... and your favorite
  teacher ... and the person that everyone laughed at ... and the person that
  has hurt you ...
And the Lord stands in the middle of the circle and tells you that this is
  his family ...
And asks everyone ... can all of you be my family together? ...
Look around for a few minutes at the people the Lord has gathered ...
Can Jesus' family be your family? ... Can all these people be your
  brothers and sisters? ...

And then suddenly everyone else disappears, only you and the Lord remain ...
And he takes you in his arms and tells you how proud he is of you,
  and that he will never leave you ...
No matter what ... he will always be with you ...
He moves to stand behind you again ... with his hand still on your shoulder ...
You can't see him anymore ...
But you know that he is still there ...
He removes his hand from your shoulder and you can't even feel him ...
But he promises that he will always be with you ...
Even if you can't see him or feel him ... he'll always be there ...
  no matter what ...
He will never leave you ... never ...
Is there anything you want to say to the Lord? ...
Anything you want to do? ...

Think about all the things that you have seen today ...
Remember all the things that you have felt ...
Hear again all the things that you have heard with your ears ...
And be aware of your arms ...
And your hands ...
Hands that God has used so many times ...
And be aware of your legs ...

And your feet, feet that God has traveled with for so long …
Be at peace …

When you are ready to come back …
Know that you are here …
With people who love you and care for you …
When you are ready, open your eyes …
I ask you not to talk for a few moments …
Just relax and think about what you have just experienced …
And be at peace …
Peace.

Meditation Nineteen

The Prayer in the Garden

We struggle to remain "awake" and alert at the time of Jesus' agony. In that agony we discover our ability, because of God's gift, to minister to the disciples and to Jesus. We then become empowered to minister to others in our life. Inspired by Luke 22:39-46. The use of relaxation technique two is suggested. Time: 12 minutes

And we pray:
Almighty God in heaven …
There are times when our path seems confusing …
When the direction we take is uncertain … when the course we should choose
    is unclear …
We get confused because we're not sure how things will work out …
Or what the future holds …
Or what we can do now to make things better later …
We try to trust in you …
We want to put our faith in you …
But that can be scary … when we're not certain of your will for us …
    when we're unsure of what is best …
As we meditate … send us your Holy Spirit to guide us … to teach us …
That we might learn deeper trust …
Deeper faith …
That we might act with greater love …
Greater hope …

With your eyes still closed …
Take a slow deep breath …
Let it fill you …
And again … another breath …
Slowly and deeply …
A breath which makes you lighter and lighter …
When you feel weightless …
Exhale the air slowly … silently …
Letting the air propel you … back in time …
Far away in the distance …
To ancient Israel … to the time of Jesus Christ …
It's early evening …
You find yourself on a high knoll …

Overlooking a valley that leads to the walled city of Jerusalem …
    ahead of you …
And in the bright moonlight you can make out the city's silhouette …
With its towers … and angled stone buildings …
Squeezed together and protected by an enormous wall …
The night air is refreshing … a cool breeze gently twists and turns …
The sky is crowded with stars … while the moon casts long shadows …
But the city seems strangely quiet … eerie …
As if something important were about to happen …
Something that no one is prepared for …

From where you are on the knoll …
You can just make out a group of travelers …
Walking from Jerusalem …
In your direction on a dirt road …
You can see that they will soon come to a fork …
When they reach it they pause …
And one of the group motions the rest to follow him into a garden …
They move through the opening of the protective stone wall … through the
    gate and into a garden … lush and peaceful … private … secluded …

And you join them there … walking with them through the old cluster of
    olive trees … trunks thick and twisted … rugged branches hanging low …
Most of the group sit under the outside edge of trees … huddled together …
    their cloaks pulled close to their chins … staying warm … getting comfortable …
The oldest of the group … Peter … points out a solitary figure over to
    one side … near a well …
Peter tells you how that man had been welcomed into Jerusalem with
    cheering … earlier in the week …
He had talked about the end being near … about how everything would
    change now … since he was coming into his kingdom …
Everyone thought he meant that he would lead a fight to get rid of the
    Romans … but he didn't … and the mood of the people began to change …
They aren't cheering anymore … and the man has many powerful enemies
    here in Jerusalem …
It's getting confusing …

Then he talked about betrayal … the man said that someone would
    betray him … one of his best friends … how could a friend betray
    another friend? …
Now we don't know who to trust …
We got into an argument … we accused each other …

He tried to bring us together for the Passover meal ... but now we suspect each other ... we are angry ...

Do you understand Peter? ... Do you know what he is trying to say about being betrayed by friends? ...
Sometimes our friends are really against us ... when we think they are supporting us ...
They can turn against us ... as if all they really cared about was themselves ...
And we become disappointed with their selfishness ... their greed ...
And become so very angry at how they ruined everything ... and we feel like we've lost all control ... and that we are at their mercy ...
Has anything like that happened to you? ...
Is there anything you would like to say to Peter? ...
Anything you could do to comfort him, soothe his hurt feelings? ...
Bring him peace ...
Peace ...

Another of the group ... the one with the reddish hair ... Thomas ... tries to explain to you how that man had said that everything would change ... now that he was leaving ...
But he won't take us with him ... he is leaving us alone ... with no way to find him ...
Thomas tells you about how he has come to depend upon this man ...
How he learned to trust him ...
How he made plans ... knowing that he would be part of those plans ...
And now he says that he is leaving ... soon he'll be gone ... and all our plans will be destroyed ... all my dreams will vanish ...

Do you understand Thomas? ... Do you know what he is trying to say about the fear of having our friends leave? ...
Our hopes fade like the morning mist ... and vanish ...
And we are left alone ... empty ... with dry tears and deep sadness ... we want to sob ... but we hurt too much ... and are drained of all our strength ...
And we become fearful about how we will continue without them ... when nothing will ever be the same ... and we know we will suffer terrible loneliness when they're gone ...
Has that ever happened to you? ...
Is there anything you would like to say to Thomas? ...
Is there any way you could comfort him? ...
Bring him peace ...
Peace ...

And then the youngest calls out for your attention … a very young
   teen-ager … John … waves you over to him …
And he begins to tell you how he wanted to help the situation …
   because he had insights … and he knew what to do …
But nobody would listen …
Nobody would pay attention to him … they just ignored him … because he
   was the youngest … they thought he didn't know anything … they took
   him for granted … even though he was the only one that
   really understood …
Nobody would give him credit or acknowledge him …
And John … with great frustration … suddenly crosses his arms over
   his chest …
As if closing himself off … as if protecting himself from more hurt …
   from being ignored …

Can you understand John? … Do you know what he is trying to say about
   being ignored or not having your opinions respected? …
Think about how you feel when people won't accept your knowledge or
   experience … and you become very frustrated …
And they treat you as if you are insignificant …
Saying that you'll know better when you get older …
And until then … they continue to treat you as if you were invisible …
Or maybe they pretend that they are listening or agreeing … but all the
   time … they're just trying to pacify you … because they think they have
   the right answer in spite of you …
And you want to tell them how ignorant they are … but it wouldn't matter …
   because they surely wouldn't listen to that either …
Has anything like that ever happened to you? …
Is there anything you could say to John? …
Is there any way you could comfort him? …
And be at peace …
Peace …

As the group becomes drowsy … yawning … falling asleep … snoring …
You slowly walk over to the solitary man … who is at a distance …
   near the well …
And as you quietly approach him from behind …
You notice that the heavy robe he wears is soaked with sweat …
   his hair is dripping … stringy and matted …
He rubs his hands together … twisting and turning them in his anxiety …
His breathing is erratic … alternately deep and shallow …
   breathing in gulps or sips …

You stand next to him ...
He looks up with his bloodshot eyes ... skin shining in the moonlight ...
   his lip trembling ... and he begins to shiver ...
Tears have streaked his face ...
And he tells you that he is scared ...
Scared ...

Nothing has seemed to work out the way that he had wanted it ...
His friends seem to have forgotten everything he said to them about
   the kingdom ...
They fight and quarrel ... argue over who is the greatest ...
Money and possessions are more important than anything ...
He had hoped to change people's hearts ... end fighting and cruelty ...
   establish God's justice ... usher in God's return to his world ... this world ...
And now ... at the end ... hoping to find healing love in the hearts of those
   around him ... he instead finds overwhelming sin ...
And he wonders if he has done something wrong ... he fears he has
   failed miserably ...
He's afraid he is a disappointment to his heavenly Father ...
And there is no time left to change things ...
And he would rather have another chance ... or more time ...
But his only choice seems to be to pay the price for all the sin that remains ...
   to suffer for those who still sin ... to take that sin upon himself and
   destroy it by letting his own life be destroyed ...
He has to die ...

"If only there were another way," he says ...
"Some way other than suffering because of others ...
Bearing all the pain that they have caused ...
Suffering the rejection even of those who claim to love me ...
My friends abandon me when I need them most ...
I don't think that I am strong enough to endure all that" ...

And Jesus begins to sob ... his hands shaking, hiding his face ...
   as if he were humiliated to have you see him at this
   difficult hour of his life ...
You can hear him murmur that there is no other way ... and that somehow
   he will just have to trust ... to surrender to the Father ... to trust that
   God the Father can make sense of whatever seems confusing ...
Then he looks up ... exhausted ... bone weary ... hand trembling ...
He extends his hand to you ... silently ... waiting ... hoping ...
Is there anything you would like to say to the Lord? ...

Is there anything you can do for him? …
Can you bring him peace? …
Peace …

Know that you'll have to let go …
You'll have to let Jesus continue on his own …
To fulfill the mystery of his earthly life as the Father has led him … alone …
But know that he continues on with the gift of your spirit …
    your caring and concern …
Know that you have an incredible ability to comfort others …
    to give people strength … because of what you have endured yourself …

Bring that gift of caring for others with you … and with stillness in your
    heart … return back here …
Leave the garden at the Mount of Olives …
And return here …
Knowing that you are not alone …
Knowing that you are with others …
Others with the same ability …
Able to offer you the kind of caring and support that you need from them …
And be at peace …

When you are ready you may open your eyes …
But please don't speak to anyone …
Or distract anyone from reflecting on the power they have to comfort
    people in their time of need …
In their time of need …
Their need for you.

Meditation Twenty

Resurrection

By remaining in vigil at the Lord's side as he rests in the tomb, we discover the power of "remembering him," his powerful movements in our lives, and the course of his Spirit in us. With dawn comes the experience of the risen Lord, who takes up a new residence deep within us. Inspired by Luke 24: 1-12. The use of relaxation technique three is suggested. Time: 15 minutes

And we pray:
Eternal God …
In your constant care and love …
You teach us by drawing us into your wisdom …
You re-create us in your image and likeness …
But the many distractions of the world often get in our way …
We lose sight of your plan and your will …
As we meditate this day …
Send us your Holy Spirit …
And your gift of remembering …
That the spirit we return may be one of cooperation …
That we might participate most fully in your divine plan …

With your eyes still closed …
Search …
Search throughout ancient Israel … for a very secluded place …
    a place of abandonment … the place where nearly everyone that had
    followed Christ finally left him … where they ultimately deserted him …
    and left his remains …
Search throughout ancient Israel for the final resting place of Jesus …
    his tomb …

Scan across the wide, parched deserts … over the rippling sea of Galilee …
    past the River Jordan snaking through lush greens and palm trees …
Down the dusty streets of Jerusalem … empty streets … silent streets …
Look to the outskirts of Jerusalem … to the hill of the skull … where three
    crosses stand empty … the blood soaked earth is once again parched and
    cracked … the crowds have departed …
Look for a nearby garden … enclosed and protected by thick thorn bushes …
    with a central well … flat and open like a pool …

141

Toward the outer edge of this garden ... a huge rock stands before an opening
    carved into the cliff ... and seals tight the tomb ...
You can enter the tomb if want to ... just relax ... let yourself move slowly
    toward the rock that blocks the entrance ... and then slowly move through
    the rock ... as if it were no more than a shadow or a dense fog ...

Now you are standing within the tomb ... the light is faint ...the darkness
    nearly complete ... you can feel the cool stone and earth beneath your feet ...
To the side ... in the back ... you can just see the body of Jesus ...
    covered with a thin sheet of linen ... a lifeless body lying completely still ...
You kneel ... silently ... alone ... and safe ... keeping vigil ...
Open your heart to the feelings of having lost someone who loved you
    very much ... a deep emptiness settles over you as if your own soul has
    been stripped and killed ... a deep and formless void of darkness covers
    everything within you ... everything outside of you ...
You kneel beside the body of Jesus ... helpless ... remembering ...
    keeping the past alive with memories ...
Wonderful ... living memories ... of a time that was ... a time that you wish
    could be alive now ... if only as a shadow of what you knew before ...

Memories ... of Jesus ...
When he first came to you ... in a way that you'll never forget ...
    touching your life so deeply ... so profoundly ...
And remember ... the first time that God seemed real to you ...
    when your faith leapt ... and worries vanished ... and you felt a certainty
    for the first time ... a confidence in God ...
Remember a time when you felt face to face with Jesus ...
    heart to heart with God ... when your soul was touched by Christ ...
Can you remember what you wanted to say to the Lord then? ...
Can you remember how he responded? ...

You were at peace ... together ... and the world stopped for a moment ...
    and you felt harmony and balance and peace ...
Hold on to that peace once more ...
Keep that peace alive within you now ...
Never let it die ...
Peace ... the eternal gift from Jesus ... a gift from God ...
Peace ...

But now ... before you ...the body of Jesus lies still ... silent ... lifeless ...
    lying flat on a cold slab of rock ...
Covered with a light cloth ... motionless ... drained of all life ...
    drained of all sorrow and pain ... a life completed ... ended ...

142

Can you remember a time when you felt deserted ... alone ...
    abandoned ... forgotten? ...
A time when you were seeking companionship ... someone to care ...
But you felt like you didn't really matter to anyone ...
And then ... deep within ... you began to sense the presence of another
    person ... your feelings of isolation were broken by the knowledge that
    God was with you ...

Remember a time when all you had to do was close your eyes to find the
    friendship of Jesus in your heart ... a time when you knew that he would
    never betray you ... a time when it was easy to find the friendship of
    the Lord ... strongly present ... close ...
When Jesus ... would give you comfort ... would ease your loneliness ...
    would be gentle with you ...
And you felt satisfied with your friendship ... certain that he would never
    leave you ... that he would stay with you always to protect you and help you ...
Remember the feelings of satisfaction you had ... of completion ...
    the sense that everything would be alright ... that you would never
    need to worry again ...

Don't let the memories of that satisfaction die ...
Don't let those feelings of comfort vanish ...
Hold on to those memories ... keep faithful to the promises that the Lord
    made with you ...
Let them continue to live ... to fill you ... energize you ... give you vitality ...
Hold firm to the promises of the Lord ...
The Lord ... the same Lord who now lies next to you in this tomb ...
    who has given up his Spirit ... silently and peacefully ...
Jesus lies here ... who was tried and convicted by sin ...
    who willingly accepted humiliation ... the humiliation of being
    stripped naked ... and nailed ... and lashed ... to a wooden cross ...
Jesus lies here ... who choked on hate ... and was pierced by fear ...
Jesus lies here ... whose life has been snuffed out ...
Only an empty shell remains ...

And you alone remain awake ... waiting ... holding vigil ...
    refusing to let go of a single memory ...
Reminiscing on those times that the Lord ... so unexpectedly ...
    touched you ... met you in a moment of sacredness ... and brought
    you incredible peace ...
Reminiscing on a time of intense anxiety ... a time when a mistake you made
    caused you to feel guilt ... a guilt that seemed too heavy to bear ...

You were caught between the humiliation of admitting the mistake ...
    and the stress of allowing the guilt to grow ... to multiply ...
    to overwhelm you ...
Until the Lord surprised you once more ...
Until he taught you how easy it is for him to forgive and forget ...
Until he taught you how to bring his forgiveness inside ... how to
    forgive yourself in the same way that he always forgives you ...
To forgive ... and forget ... to let it go ... to begin life anew ... fresh ... whole ...
To be healed by God's forgiving love ...
Until the Lord touched and healed ...
Made your burden light ... gave you more freedom than you had ever
    had before ... and created with you a sacred moment ... when heaven and
    earth touched ... and the forgiveness of heaven crushed the sin of earth ...
    destroyed it ... so that sin could never destroy life again ...
Can you remember what you wanted to say to the Lord then? ...
Can you remember how he responded? ...

He has promised that sin will never destroy life again ... as Jesus has been
    crushed by sin ... destroyed ... and left here before you ...
If the world depended upon your prayer ... if the future of all the world
    hinged upon your ability to pray ... to connect with the heart of God ...
What would you want God to know? ...
What would you say? ...
What shape would your prayer take? ...
Express what is in your heart ...
Slowly ... and silently ... let God know what is inside of you ...
    what needs to be expressed ...
And be at peace ... with God ...
Peace ...

You know that God in heaven must weep ... heartbroken by the death of Jesus ...
    think how God's heart must be broken ... pouring out divine love
    for Jesus ...
And in that tomb ... silently ... and alone ... you begin to sense a
    strange energy ... an intensity you have never before experienced ...
The entire tomb is filled with something electric ... an energy in the darkness
    that engulfs the body of Christ ...
You watch in amazement as God pours out divine energy ... divine love ...
    into Jesus ...
Love that fills ... saturates ... penetrates even death ...
Love that gives new life ...

And there ... within the tomb ... the ultimate miracle ... the ultimate
  divine life ...
You can see the eyes of Jesus begin to blink ... his eyes releasing tears of joy ...
  he stretches ... bends his fingers ... stretches again ... and stands ...
The power of God's love ... the energy of divine life ... has given the body of
  the Lord a new quality ... he is transformed ... different ... the same Jesus ...
  but something incredible has happened ... he has been changed ...
And the Lord smiles ... confident ...

Suddenly you are both aware of how incredibly free Christ is now ... free to
  complete ... in new ways ... his work of establishing God's kingdom ...
And Jesus the Christ ... whispers quietly to you ... thanks you for your
  faith ... faith that kept you close to him ... even in the hour of his death ...
  faith that kept you waiting in vigil ...
The Lord promises you a new gift ... the gift of his new life ...
  the promise of his being with you always ...
And Jesus steps behind you ...
You can't see him anymore ... but you know that he is still there ...
You can't feel him anymore ... but you are certain that he hasn't left you ...

And suddenly ... Jesus takes a step forward ... stepping into you ...
And you can feel ... a new presence of God ...
Jesus ... steps his foot into yours ... slides his leg into yours ...
It is almost like putting on gloves ... Jesus slides his hand into your hand ...
  his arms into your arms ...
He steps into you ... becoming part of you ...
And you can feel his heart ... touching your heart ... becoming part of
  your heart ... you can feel the divinity of God becoming part of you ...
The sacred life of Christ ... entering you ... becoming part of you ...
You can feel that divine life filling you ... making you holy ... sacred ...
  worthy of heaven ... worthy of God ...

It is God who makes you sacred ... God who gives his eternal life ...
It is God who asks you to protect his sacred life ... to care for your holiness ...
  to be proud of holding within you the power of the resurrection ... of life ...
Christ who will never leave you ... is now a part of you ...
  he will re-create you ...
And be at peace ...
How can you respond to God? ...
What would you want God to know? ...
Be at peace ...

Now you notice that the stone that had been sealing the tomb has rolled away …
Before you is the brightness of a new day … a new life …
You have within you … the power of the resurrection … the presence
    of God … a presence that empowers you …
You are standing within the tomb … facing the challenges of the new life …
And Jesus, deep within you, offers you the choice … to remain in the
    safety of the tomb … alone … with him …
Or to venture into the world with him … to face all of its uncertainties …
    with a new vitality … with a new power and strength …
The choice to act in the world … or remain apart from it …
God quietly … gently … asks for your choice …
Just rest … and consider … and decide …

After you make your decision …
Come back here …
And know that you are not alone …
There are others here with you …
Others who have been given the same choice … who hold on to the
    same living memories …
Others who have been empowered by Christ …

When you are ready … you may open your eyes …
    but remain quiet and still … secluded …
To give yourself a moment to reflect … to bring back with you
    the memories and your decision …
Simply rest … and reflect …
And hold on to that peace …
The peace that only the Lord can give.

Section Three

Four Responses

Perhaps the greatest challenge to anyone who prays is to bring the movements of the Holy Spirit within the recesses of the heart out into the reality of our everyday world. With teens, this is an especially important task, since they will quickly see prayer as "a waste of time" if it does not seem to affect or connect with the reality they are living. For all of us, prayer will only be effective if we find ways to allow it to change our hearts and our lives. It must be allowed to affect what we think and feel and the way we act and live our lives.

The four exercises provided in this final section are intended to help your teens do all these things. Once the meditation is finished, choose one of these exercises to provide opportunities for reflection on the experience of the meditation, the relevance of that experience, and the effect of their ever-closer relationship with God on the patterns of relationships in their lives.

Written Prayers

The written response to the meditation prayer is perhaps the single most effective form of bringing its spiritual impact back into the everyday world. Writing helps to make the realities of the heart tangible, the movements of the Spirit concrete.

While writing is the easiest form of response for most people of most ages, it is important to remember that the brief period of time between the meditation's conclusion and the writing of the first word is critical. That's when many people are very susceptible to distractions and can easily lose any reflective thought. Therefore, paper, pens, a lapboard, anything that could be necessary or helpful to the participants should be distributed prior to the meditation. Also, be sure that all explanations are given before the meditation begins, even before the group moves to its chosen sacred space, so that there is no confusion after the meditation. Be sure to allow people whatever time they need for reflection on their prayer before writing; this may often be up to three minutes but will rarely be much longer.

I find that God's Spirit can impact the soul in a variety of profound ways. And likewise, the many ways the individual can respond to and express this impact are just as varied. The form of the writing may take the shape of a song, a lyric, a poem, or even a story. These should be suggested and certainly never discouraged. But the easiest, I have found, is most often a letter: a letter to God, to the Blessed Mother, to the Holy Spirit, or to Jesus. You might suggest a beginning to start the individual in their writing: "Dear Jesus ..." or "Dear God ..." The person can then write about whatever is happening in their heart, whatever their reflections are from the meditation.

Writing is an excellent method of moving our feelings out from the deep corners of our hearts into tangible words that can be more easily considered and evaluated. Encourage your group to let the words flow, regardless of grammar, spelling, or punctuation.

Younger students may only need to write two or three sentences. Their response usually takes the form of a quick insight or resolution. A brief request from God is also common. The more mature and experienced writer can produce volumes. Letting each person take as much or as little time as they need is usually best. The only caution is to encourage silence after the first people are finished so that they will not distract those still engaged. The results of this writing, the group's pages of prayer and reflection, can then be used as a springboard to any of the three following responses.

Response Two

Small Group Sharing

Guided meditation often allows the Holy Spirit to touch and transform the deepest recesses of the human heart. These secret places that God touches during prayer are usually the most sensitive and vulnerable spots we have. Sensing these places of weakness, most people will spend much of their time and energy protecting and masking them. Because of this, asking a person to share with others in a large group, to open these vulnerable places to the gaze of strangers, is often fearful, threatening, and downright defeating.

On the other hand, Christian witness and sharing remains a valuable means of fostering trust and promoting mutual growth. Christian community can be encouraged, and people can become sensitized to each other, providing a fertile ground for exercising the fruits of their meditations.

Unless the larger group has already had fairly extensive, fruitful experience in intimate sharing, I would strongly recommend leaving this kind of response to a smaller group. Three, four, or at most, five people are much easier to deal with than a larger number of strangers. The smaller group allows for more speedy development of trust. Even then, before the sharing of the meditation's results, an intimate confidence and security still needs to be established among the group members. Most often the second or third time a group shares together will be far more successful than the first.

Facilitators for the small groups could be handed a brief list of questions to help new groups start discussion. Questions such as these would be appropriate, although you may want to provide your own that more closely connect to the meditation you choose:

What kinds of feelings did you have during the meditation?

What insight did you find?

What do you think the Holy Spirit was trying to accomplish with you during that prayer?

What new lesson about your life could you share with someone else because of the meditation?

Why do you think everyone's experience during the same meditation is so different?

How can your everyday life be affected by this meditation?

What was the most satisfying part of the meditation?

Often, one or two of these questions, posed to the group as a whole, will be enough to generate a conversation that will take on a life of its own, growing out of the participants' experiences. There is no need for a group to attempt to answer all of these questions each time—or any of them if they are able to begin their reflection on their own. However, they are a useful resource for a new group that may not know where or how to begin.

Another option for the small group, which I find the most effective (and most challenging), is sharing the participants' letters to Jesus. This sharing can be introduced as a gift from the writer to the group. If an adequate level of trust has already been established, then there are two rules for the small group interaction which usually govern the sharing of these letters. First, no one is allowed to speak negatively or positively of someone's letter. Compliments in small groups are often judged as being greater for others than for the self, no matter how untrue that might be. Second, if one person is willing to share, then everyone else will also be expected to share. Without such a stipulation, there may be very little motivation for the building of trust among newer groups.

As an added bonus for this option, the sharing of the letters, which creates an equality of vulnerability, often leads the group into praying for each other and making mutual commitments.

Response Three

The Emmaus Walk

The Celts of Ireland in its early Christian period had a special companion who was called a soul-friend. With this person individuals would confide their spiritual struggles, growth, and challenges. The soul-friend could then offer insights, cautions, and understanding to the struggling or rejoicing Christian. The two, in fact, brought the working of the Holy Spirit to each other. Like the scriptural story of the two disciples on their way to Emmaus, they could, in their sharing of their own stories, find Jesus walking their path with them.

The model of the soul-friend or the two disciples on the road to Emmaus can effectively be used as an alternative to a small group discussion.

There are many possibilities for pairing people off. The most obvious is to let them choose their own partners. The advantage to this is that the two would already have an affinity for each other. They would also enjoy the compliment of being chosen. The disadvantage is that people who know each other usually have established roles and images for the other person. Changing those established roles and learning to see new aspects can be difficult, if not impossible. Sometimes good friends will not take the situation seriously, and especially with young people, prefer to entertain their friends hoping for their approval.

Other alternatives for establishing pairs might be to have them count off and be paired randomly, or to connect two people deliberately who are not really well known to each other. I find this latter alternative to ultimately be of greater reward, although it may initially be met with resistance. People enjoy discovering other new people, especially when, in their vulnerability, they eagerly find mutual acceptance. New relationships begin; new bonds emerge. A network of Christians is established at a very intimate level.

Activities on the walk could include the same sharing and the same questions provided to the small group facilitators. Allow approximately thirty minutes for the walk, but this may vary from pair to pair and should not be adhered to too strictly.

Response Four

The Journal

Guided meditations can become a rich resource for spiritual direction. They can give experiential form to the movement of the Spirit and become a point of reference. Therefore, keeping a written journal of the participant's experiences, insights, and resolutions that occur because of their prayer can facilitate meaningful dialogue for both the spiritual director and the person directed.

Before your group begins keeping their journals, help them to be aware how easy it is to inadvertently edit or censor the response to the meditation that they are recording. Encourage them to try not to omit some things because they might be ashamed of them or embarrassed by them. Likewise, they should avoid emphasizing those things that they are proud of. It is all too easy to slant what is being reported unrealistically without even realizing it. To do so would be a disservice both to the Spirit and to your teens. Stress with them that a neutral and completely honest position will be most productive.

One successful format for journal entry is the four-stage approach. Discussing these four steps with your teens may help them get started especially if keeping a journal is a new experience for them.

Observation. The first phase of writing is the immediate recollection of the action and what transpired during the meditation. This is bringing back to our minds the sequences of events and emotions from the active part of the prayer. How were the individuals, the actions, and the feelings connected? What were the associations?

Listening. Next is to try to identify why the Holy Spirit would have brought those particular people or emotions into the action. Can we move beyond the words of the meditation and discover Christ communicating with us? What was the Lord saying, doing, encouraging us to move toward? In the quiet of our hearts, we listen to the movement of the Spirit and then record that.

Insight. We then try to attach meaning to the meditation and discover the personal implications of it for us. Sorting it through, have we gleaned any kind of insight from the prayer? What made this meditation unique? Did we observe something that we had not realized before? What was the value Christ was uncovering for us?

Resolution. Having had the opportunity to listen to God's movement in our lives, we move toward balancing our lives with God's. When our hearts or souls have been touched by God, we are often left with some sort of experience that has a far-reaching effect. As a result of this prayer, what action or goal are we aimed at? What is the consequence of our divine encounter? How will that affect our lives? What will our response be in return?

Each journal response offers a concrete review of the personal prayer experience which can later be used for input by the director. Collectively, the journal entries become a systematic map of the Spirit's movement in a person's life, usually highlighting significant points of God's approach. Like road markers, each entry becomes one more visual step of a person's journey to God. In addition, the journal can become a great source of consolation for the participant when later reviewing it.

Although journals can be anything that saves words (from scraps of paper to computers), it is best for the journal itself to take on an important significance. It should lend itself to a sense of specialness, with secure and permanent pages. With certainty, such a piece of literature would take on greater importance throughout the individual's life and become for them a great treasure.